Finding
My
Balance

A Memoir

Mariel Hemingway

Simon & Schuster
New York   London   Toronto   Sydney   Singapore

SIMON & SCHUSTER
Rockefeller Center
1230 Avenue of the Americas
New York, NY 10020

For information regarding special discounts for bulk purchases,
please contact Simon & Schuster Special Sales at 1-800-456-6798
or business@simonandschuster.com

Designed by Laura Lindgren

Manufactured in the United States of America

10 9 8 7 6 5 4 3 2 1

Library of Congress Cataloging-in-Publication Data

Hemingway, Mariel.
    Finding my balance : a memoir with yoga / Mariel Hemingway.
        p. cm.
    1. Yoga. 2. Yoga, Haòha. I. Title.
    RA781.7.H46 2003
613.7'046—dc21   2002036543

ISBN 0-7432-3807-9

ACKNOWLEDGMENTS

I am forever grateful to Dr. Peter Evans for his unconditional love and care for me and my family. I am deeply indebted to Bill Hedden, without whom this book would still be scattered thoughts inside the pages of my journal. My profound gratitude to Michele Evans for teaching me the subtle nuances of behaving like a lady and, most important, for being my spiritual inspiration. Thank you to Mark Stephens for generously donating LA Yoga Center space and overseeing the asanas. And I especially want to thank my dear husband, Stephen, and our daughters, Dree and Langley, who weather all my storms with grace and love.

For my beloved Guru
Paramahansa Yogananda

Finding

My

Balance

MOUNTAIN POSE,
OR *TADASANA*

I want to begin this story about my life by simply standing still. Standing on our own two feet with stability and awareness is hugely important in all our lives, and it seems easy enough. I stand here, supposedly straight and stable, balanced and awake. But am I really? I rock my weight back and forth on my feet, trying to find my true center. The funny thing is that I am sure that what's center for me today was imbalance yesterday, or will be tomorrow. But forget that. I make a commitment to nothing except my willingness to be present on my own feet, inside my body, today—right now.

The premise of Mountain pose, like all standing yoga postures, is to stimulate the body and the mind. I tense my thigh muscles and release them, and after that release I seek a comfortable holding position that feels invigorating without tension. Concentrating on the sensation, I try to bring all the muscles in my body into this pleasant state, while standing in this apparently simple posture. I find that it is not at all a simple thing to do. There are complexities to my body even while I am standing still. Am I making a line of my crown, ears, and ankles? Are my sides extended evenly, with the same length, depth, and intensity? I pull my spine up out of my waist, feeling lightness in the intention of a straight body. My neck is long and an extension of my long spine. I spread my toes to find my solid ground. *Ah yes!* That reminds me of the importance of my feet. Solid contact with the earth is the root of this posture.

As I reflect on Mountain pose and understand the implications of its name, I can begin to understand my great need for stability and groundedness. Something about stability is so appealing to me in a world where I find it very difficult to feel solid on my feet, or even to feel that I'm inside my body! I think this goes way back for me. Probably, like a lot of people, my sense of instability came from a childhood where too many things were turned upside down. Caring for a sick mother in a ravaged family, I became the parent at a time when *I* needed reassurance and mothering.

My childhood home in Ketchum was across Idaho's Big Wood River and a few miles upstream from the cabin where my grandfather Ernest had lived. He killed himself with a shotgun just four months before I was born—the fourth suicide in his immediate family. Was it a genetic predisposition to depression and alcoholism, or an unhealthy family environment that produced disastrous emotional habits? Whatever the cause, it's the kind of family album that gets you thinking. Continued tragedies in succeeding generations of our family have left me coping with a full slate of problems and fears every day in my life. Finding my own answers has come to seem like a matter of survival. That struggle has shaped me. It is the story I want to tell.

My heartbreakingly lovely mother, Byra Louise Whittlesey, or Puck, as she was called, had been married once before she met my father, to a handsome aviator who flew off into World War II right after the wedding and never returned. She was left with an unfading fantasy of perfect romance. In contrast, her relationship with my dad quickly became all too real, and dreams of romance faded. That made our house a loveless and unhappy one. My parents met in Sun Valley soon after the end of the war. Mom was working as an administrator for United Airlines, a mourning widow who was too tall to be a stewardess. At the Sun Valley Lodge she ran into a handsome young bellhop named Jack Hemingway. He quickly fell head over heels for the striking, dark-haired guest with the chiseled bone structure and gorgeous legs. She wasn't an easy catch, though. Her heart was broken, and even had she been willing to share it, there were lots of other suitors. Dad pursued her for four years before she broke down, deciding that a life of travel and adventure with him was better than a life in mourning. It might not have been the best basis for a marriage; I think my mother was never in love with Dad, and he never felt loved by her.

Mom never really consented to her marriage—that reality came out in scores of little ways in our family. Though

Mom and Dad on their wedding day.

she was good at domestic affairs, she resented everything she had to do around the house. I can recall her in
her old clothes, powering through the chores with a bucket
of cleaning products and rags. The vacuum hummed.
But if I walked into the house after she mopped the floor,
she would scream, "Take off your damn shoes," or simply
whack my arm and growl. This was not cleaning with a
smile.

Mother was a great cook, but she seemed to cook only to prove how unappreciated she was. Every day, she would plan an exotic meal for dinner, like Cuban-style *picadillo* or Italian food with handmade pasta. She was an artist, but all during the beautiful process she would be cursing about how her goddamn husband would pour salt all over the food without even tasting, or go off to eat cheese and crackers after dinner was over. She always cooked, and she was always pissed off at my dad about food. Meals at our house were a time for feeling uncomfortable, and we went off separately afterward to nurse our poor digestion. Today, with my own family, I always try to add more love than talent to my cooking, believing that the loving atmosphere at the table is the most important ingredient.

In 1970, when I was eight, our family suffered its first big shock. Dad, the tennis player and outdoorsman, had a severe heart attack in his forties. No doubt, his abuse of cigarettes and alcohol exacted a toll on him, but I've always thought that his heart gave out because it was broken. He couldn't handle constant rejection by the woman he loved. In any case, he l anded in the Sun Valley Hospital for a month, heavily dosed with drugs. The drugs seemed to work on him like some kind of evil truth serum, and he became hostile toward Mom, telling her how neglected he felt. He recklessly plunged into a blatant affair with one of the nurses. Mom was suddenly vulnerable and emotional at home. She tried to hide her embarrassment, but that is nearly impossible in a small town, especially when you have a bevy of interested daughters. Everybody seemed to know everything about our little domestic scandal.

My christening with Dad, Margaux, Mom, and Muffet

Dad came home from the hospital with doctor's marching orders for the lot of us. He was to avoid stress at all costs, so we were warned to be on our best behavior, or we would threaten his health. No more smoking, which meant Mom had to quit, too. And his diet was to be low-fat from now on, a change that replaced butter on our table with the despised margarine. Yuck! Mom rebelled quietly, but resolutely. When Dad was napping in the afternoon and my sisters were off at school, she would disappear into the closet-sized laundry room to "secretly" smoke. Once, I remember rounding the corner looking for her, baby doll in my arms, only to meet her emerging from the bathroom followed by billowing clouds of smoke. She had a matter-of-fact look on being caught, and responded to my wide-eyed disapproval with a simple "What?!" It was clear she

Muffet, Margaux, and me.

wanted no answer when she slapped my bottom and pushed me into the kitchen. There was to be no talk about the foggy bathroom, ever. "The hell with him," she would say under her breath.

Dad quickly got over his affair, but the damage to their marriage mounted daily. We were always tense. Dinners got so bad that we gave up the kitchen altogether and took to eating my mother's gourmet cooking in front of *To Tell the Truth* or *Jeopardy!* Life spiraled into a dull hell. The center of my family life at home was the older of my two sisters, Muffet. She was eleven years older than I, and made me feel more loved and cared for than anyone else did. When she was home, she would pick me up from school and drive twisting down the road like a snake. While I shrieked with laughter, she would explain that I should never get sun on my face or squint if I wanted to avoid wrinkles. She would hold her beautiful face exquisitely still to demonstrate. But Muffet disengaged from the awful family dynamic. Off on her own, she developed a dark secret, one that is painfully obvious in hindsight. She escaped to spend a lot of time during the sixties in northern California, hanging out at Grateful Dead concerts. I recall my mother berating her for her velvet capes, dark lipstick, striped bell-bottoms, and bare feet. She was screamed at for her detached attitude and disrespectful behavior. My confusion mounted as this beloved free spirit got into chilling rages aimed at my parents. None of us had any clue that she was often tripping on LSD.

I particularly recall one day when I was eleven. I had come home from school, eaten masses of celery with peanut butter, and gone out to the backyard to jump on my trampoline. I was jumping and back flipping, trying to touch the clouds with my fingertips, when I heard yelling from inside the house. Unlike the usual yelling of a volatile family, this was incredibly urgent—so urgent that I bounced to the ground and ran for the house. Inside, my mother and Muffet were fighting near the stairway. I could distinguish two different sounds in the ruckus. Mom was trying to calm Muffet down, talking gently and quietly, while my sister was screaming obscenities about a fictitious life as an artist in Paris. She said she needed to get back to her roots there. I didn't know about her roots, but she had just returned from studying at the Sorbonne, where she had perfected her French. She was wildly claiming to be a painter and the lover of Picasso, alternating between English and French, all in a scream. I was surprised that my mother, whose back was toward me, was being so submissive; it was not her style at all to back down when being confronted. But she sounded terrified.

I moved closer to see if I could help break up the fight, and from my new position I could see that Muffet was threatening Mom with a pair of scissors held inches from her face. I didn't know what to do—scream, grab Muffet, run away, or call the police—so I stood there motionless. But my mother wasn't so helpless. She said, in a trembling but reasonable voice, "Look, Muffet, Mariel is behind you. You're scaring her." It was completely true. I was terrified. As Muffet turned to look at me, Mom grabbed the scissors from her hand. Disarmed, Muffet melted into tears, as did Mom. I joined them. I didn't understand at all what had happened or why. It later fell to Dad to explain to me that Muffet had taken LSD, and it caused her brain to "get nutty," as he described it.

The acid triggered a chemical imbalance in her. She once claimed that her calling in life was to fly—actually fly—and clothes restricted her. She threatened to hurt my mother if she stopped her from expressing her true nature. So, she ran naked through the streets of Ketchum. My parents were at a complete loss and eventually had her sent away to a neural institution for a few months. I didn't know where she had gone, but I missed her terribly. She was the painter, cook, and haircutter who made home seem like home. For my parents, she was not only a problem but an embarrassment within the community. They told me she had some sort of physical illness. It was several years before wiser doctors and loving friends helped Muffet discover that her condition was treatable with a careful regimen of therapeutic drugs and emotional support.

My other sister, Margaux, was seven years older than I, already starting to show her supermodel beauty when the family began to fall apart. Rebelling against Mom and Dad, she became the youngest patron of the Pioneer Bar in town, at the age of fourteen. She was completely wild. School nights were no different from the weekend for her. No curfew, no amount of parental screaming held her back. She partied all weekend on the ski hills, filling her bota bag with wine or tequila and fearlessly bolting down double Black Diamond runs stoned and drunk. Angry resort security people regularly had to escort her off the mountain. She gave up on school and rarely went a whole week without getting into major trouble. The stress on our parents was going through the roof. As soon as Margaux's modeling career took off, she left home to party on the road.

All in all, my mom's attitude and emotional distance left me, as the baby of the family, with no role model to help me understand the feminine side of my personality. This has been a constant problem in my life. What is a woman supposed to do? How is she supposed to act? As a kid, I frantically tried to clean the house, hoping that by being extra good I could somehow heal everything. It didn't work, so I developed my escape routines like everybody else.

I grew up a tomboy, skiing and hiking; so before there was yoga and Mountain pose, there were mountains. The beauty of the Sawtooth Range was a comforting gift to me. When I could drive—and country kids in Idaho drive at the age of fourteen—I would head off alone to places where the steep hills came right down near the road. I climbed dusty trails and boulder-filled avalanche chutes up to the high places. The cool mountain air was a blessed contrast to the overheated atmosphere of home. I would propel my body upward, making a mental pact with myself that if I could just get to the top of the ridge or the peak, all the anxiety that consumed me would fall away. It usually worked, too. Arriving at the top, with my lungs and thighs burning, I would look out and feel things start to sort themselves out, fall into perspective. The muscles of the mountains comforted me, literal rocks to hold on to, so unlike the instability of my home. I would run and skip down, smelling the bruised sage and the dying smell of summer gone by. To this day, I look lovingly at the familiar view behind my home, deeply comforted because the mountains never change, no matter how the weather and environment swirl around them.

Eventually, though, I had to come down from the security of the peaks. I had the dubious honor of going to school at Ernest Hemingway Elementary, where the kids called me "rich bitch" and kicked me while we stood in the pay phone line. Many of them believed I owned the school and all were sure I was somehow getting special treatment. I wanted to explain that the only connection we Hemingways had to the school was that my grandmother made a donation for the hardwood floor in the gym, but the words wouldn't come. I just held back my tears and prayed for graduation.

Dad's feelings of being unloved surely got a huge boost when Papa Ernest killed himself. The effect of a suicide is devastating on those left behind. I'm certain Dad felt deeply abandoned and uncared for, but he kept his emotions to himself. It really must have been too much when he couldn't win the love of his wife. He escaped our unhappy home by practically living out of doors, fishing and hunting his way across the world. I cherished the times he took me fishing with him in the northern Rockies, or on Pacific steelhead streams. Through him, I learned to love the outdoors, though our times together weren't overtly emotionally demonstrative. Somehow, he couldn't directly communicate his love for me, so he revealed his feelings through an intense and competitive athletic relationship. When I played soccer or ran to train for ski racing, he would always tell me that he ran farther still. If I hiked, he would say he had hiked and played tennis, too. I always felt that he was proving that he was better than me. I didn't understand until much later that it was his confused way of showing love.

For obvious reasons, Dad almost never mentioned his famous father. I had to discover the writings of Ernest Hemingway by myself. Like most students, I first picked up *The Old Man and the Sea*. I was eleven and a slow reader, and I was afraid that I wouldn't understand the book; but the deep, simple prose carried me off far into the night, out on the ultramarine waters off Cuba with Santiago. I finished a big-person book in two sittings! I felt that I understood my grandfather, knew for the first time that he really was my family. We shared the same blood. I felt I understood him better than anybody else. It was the beginning of my love of books.

Margaux rarely took time out from her wild life to visit us, but when she did, she left me wide-eyed with her beauty and reckless sense of fun. As soon as I became a teenager she wangled me a part in the movie *Lipstick*, in which she had the starring role. I was so innocent when the film began that I didn't even understand that my character was raped in the movie. Off the set, though, I was being forced to grow up pretty fast. Mother was diagnosed with cancer that year, 1975, and I truly came to feel that there was nobody who would take care of me if I didn't do it myself. When *Lipstick* was released, people said I was a star, while Margaux's acting was hurtfully panned. She intensified her self-destructive behavior, and the distance between us began to take on adult dimensions.

Soon after my mother's cancer was diagnosed, the family was shocked when Muffet, who had controlled her illness well enough to fall in love and get married, suffered a series of mental breakdowns. She simply couldn't be persuaded to take her medicine. Her marriage collapsed and she returned home to the care of my mother, who was herself undergoing chemotherapy and radiation treatments. That was when I began a long pattern of living in fear that I would become ill like my mother or go crazy like my sisters.

I choose to believe that many children are put in difficult situations in life so they will be challenged to grow and become stronger. My situation certainly propelled me to search for love and stability in my life, though the propulsion began like a Chinese rocket, shooting all over the place.

I'll get into that wild ride soon enough, but for now let's return to the yoga mat, where I am standing as straight and still and aware as I can be on this day. I have squeezed and maneuvered and played with all my muscles so I can find the solid, peaceful, unscathed mountain that is me. Here I find the silence.

2

TRIANGLE POSE,
OR *UTTHITA TRIKONASANA*

Truly, after Mountain pose I realize that
I am looking to find that same stability in every other pose,
or asana, that I will do in my practice. It is the dependable
foundation I can build on. So, I am still standing on my
two grounded feet, which are now spread apart, the right
directed to the right and the left at forty-five degrees, pointing forward. Stretching my arms out, I shift the weight of
my torso from center to the right, and find the floor on the
outside of my right foot with my right hand. If I am tight,
I just hold my ankle. In this position I must first make
sure that my feet still have the same anchored feeling they
had while I was standing upright. Once I feel that, I look
upward into my left hand, stretched toward the sky. This is
the Triangle pose, another invigorating and stabilizing standing pose.

Now the wiggling and adjusting begins. I feel my feet and spread my toes, solidifying the base again. I tense the muscles of my legs and release them, bringing them into a gentle engagement that pulls my thighs up. Strangely, doing this gives me a feeling of lightness in the pose. Next, I check to make sure my ribs aren't collapsing down toward my thigh on the right side, and that I am not allowing them to pop forward. It's a delicate game that is easy to be lax with. My arms are outstretched and aligned all the way to the fingertips, and my shoulders are pulled out of my ears. I stretch my spine, vertebra by vertebra, from the coccyx all the way to my neck. Sometimes I'm unable to look up toward my left hand because my neck hurts, so I simply look down periodically at my right foot. No big deal. I know never to do anything if it is hurting or uncomfortable. But did I always know this? Of course not!

I was a ski racer from the age of seven until I was fifteen. During training, we all learned and believed that the pain was what made us stronger and more competitive. In truth, though, it made me feel insecure and long for freedom from the pain and pressure. I know from watching my own daughters that girls view competition and challenge as part of playing, but far too few of them learn that competing is fun and joyous, whether you win or lose. I certainly didn't know that, and when I competed at skiing or tennis, I lost the sense of fun.

Skiing scared me completely. My stomach was always so upset that I took antacids and suffered diarrhea, always wanting to dash from the starting gate back to the bathroom. I was good at dual slaloms, where I raced head-to-head with another girl, but the races took their toll on my stomach. The direct competition filled me with dread. I recall one beautiful day in Sun Valley when I raced a teammate and casual friend. We rode the chairlift to the top of the mountain together. She didn't look like a friend before the race, though. She looked angry and intimidating. I wanted to beg my way out of the race and take her for some hot chocolate at the lodge, where we could laugh together in front of the fire.

Instead, we were poised in the gate as the countdown ticked off—ten-nine-eight-seven-six-five—*Oh God, I hate this*—four—*I'm gonna get sick*—three—*Can I go home? Please save me*—two, and one—and I kicked out with a blast of power. The first three gates blurred past me without a further thought, my body taking over. I even managed to hit the gates with my shoulder as I built speed. It actually felt good. Then I started to think—which was a bad idea—that things were going well. I could hear the other girl catching up and see the tips of her skis out of the corner of my left eye. My stomach cramped again. The next gate was very tight and I sliced over the ice and ruts feeling that I would be OK if I could just keep focused. But I could feel her closer and closer to me—out of her course! The instant I passed the next gate, she snagged her ski on it, going into a cartwheel that ripped her ski into mine. My tip caught the next-to-last gate, throwing me on my back in perfect time to catch her flying ski on my face. After we both slid to a stop, we lay motionless for a long time until I could feel the blood dripping from a big gash beside my nose. I still have the scar from that forty-stitch cut. It reminds me that when the race is over and the helicopter ride to the hospital is flown, there is still a race next weekend to face.

That same belief in sweaty, painful exercise carried over into my early yoga experiences, casually in 1976, seriously by 1985. If it didn't hurt so much that I couldn't wait for it to be over, it wasn't for me. So I was naturally drawn to Bikram yoga, which builds strength, balance, and flexibility in a roasting-hot, sweaty room. I loved the hard workout, and found that it was a major challenge to my mind as well as to my body. Since I was so dedicated, I advanced quickly and was soon taking classes in Los Angeles from Bikram himself. He sat shirtless in a Speedo on red velvet cushions arranged like a throne. In his hand was a Coke or Pepsi to help fend off the 110-degree heat. When he spoke, his voice was very loud and jolting, and usually challenging or mocking. It was a daunting class. Beside me I could see the gorgeous silhouette of Juliet Prowse, whose postures were so beautiful and inspiring. I think she was the reason I stayed in the class as long as I did.

Eventually, Bikram brought his attention to me. I have always been very flexible but not terribly strong. He took all that in immediately and began taunting me. He said I thought I was so good and so flexible, but I couldn't hold the postures. I was humiliated. The last thing I wanted was for him to single me out. I didn't think I was any good at all. I went back to his class half a dozen times, but I could never get past his teasing. You must understand that my goals were mostly external: striving for performance and weight loss and the approval of my teachers. Trying to please the critical master on the outside and the even more demanding voice on the inside of my head, I injured myself by pushing too hard, going beyond my boundaries, and I had to give up yoga for a while. I now know that the aggressive-teacher approach helps some students, though it doesn't work for me. When I do Bikram yoga today, I always seek out a teacher who guides the class in a loving way.

The bad experience kept me away from yoga for years, until a friend told me that Power Yoga would kick my butt. My ego trapped me again! I laughed at the challenge, knowing that I could climb a mountain in the time it took my friend to think about doing it. So I arrogantly arrived at Bryan Kest's very packed Power Yoga class at Yoga Works, and promptly got my butt kicked. The amount of time we spent in Downward Facing Dog pose amazed me. It felt like a lifetime to my arms. I didn't realize that the strength comes from the belly, or center, so I was just propping everything up on my exhausted arms. The class seemed to hold every pose longer than I could manage, and then move into another difficult one without any rest. That sequence is supposed to be the great beauty of Power Yoga, building heat, strength, and focus. Instead, my arms were shaking during Down Dog and my thighs burning in Warrior. When we went into the push-up pose of Chaturanga, I was toast. I guess my celebrity attracted attention, since it certainly was not the graceful way I went from pose to pose. Anyway, the teacher was watching, so I continued to throw myself into the exhausting routine and ended up with my ego chattering away at me. Either I had to pretend that yoga did not exist or I had to master it.

I had no concept of what hatha yoga meant except on the most physical level. My powers of observation were directed to watching everybody else rather than watching myself. But, by taking the classes daily, my strength and balance finally began to catch up to my overly flexible body. I was hooked. I thought of yoga initially as merely a workout, sweating profusely and using my physical exhaustion to drive the demons out of my head. The thing I wasn't wholly conscious of was the quiet I was beginning to experience inside myself.

At first, I thought it was just the exhaustion—I was never the one in class to sit back in Rabbit pose when my body was screaming. But in my quest for getting or keeping the perfect thin body, I began to hear inspiring, slightly confusing words, like "This is your practice—only for you." "Quit watching the person next to you; they don't have your body, your day, or your pain." And, "If you were just to breathe with attention for a full hour, you would benefit your body, mind, and spirit far more than any of the yoga postures could teach you."

I began to listen to yoga's messages, and that taught me to listen to myself. Although I still pushed into performance places, I was slowly feeling different about many things. I no longer needed yoga only for my body. I sorely needed it for my mind. By practicing the art of being aware and present, I was learning how movement through space could lead to a stillness in the body, and more important, to a stillness in the brain. What started out as exhaustion of my body to temper my fears and demons became a most exquisite remedy for the noise that was, and is, in my head. So now, with my own yoga practice, I have learned and taught myself to play again, this time without judgment from me or the outside world.

Triangle pose, because of its lopsided transition from the strong, solid base in *Tadasana* (standing/Mountain), has a lot of what life throws at us, the daily surprises that drag us away from center. Beginning from relative stability, I lean my torso over to the side, shifting my center and my brain. This can throw me off balance, or I can continue to engage the center without squeezing, making contact with my roots—my feet and legs. A little playful exploration and I can find balance, peace, and comfort in the pose. Of course, if my muscles are screaming at me on a particular day, this is much easier said than done. To help students through these moments, yoga instructors sometimes say that the bones of our bodies are like our souls, and the muscles like our minds. What that means for me is that the bones can ground us and be solid without interference, like our souls, which are essentially nonconfrontational and peaceful; but the muscles, like the mind, chatter at us.

My mind is always throwing me off balance with thoughts that are not rooted in the present moment. I think of my kids' school schedules, or how my body does not fit the perfect image I have of myself. The muscles are the same: *I'm tight. I can't hold this. I'm tearing.* The noise goes on and on. I just try to observe these complaining muscles. I never hold a posture in pain, but see if I can find a somewhat comfortable place where I can just listen without letting the voices of the muscles take over. As long as there is no pain, I can watch how the noise dissipates and I find some moments of peace. This is tremendous practice for life. It is the practice of taking time out before reacting to all that the mind conjures up to throw me off balance.

3

RABBIT POSE

Rabbit, or child's pose, is a simple resting pose that can truly rejuvenate my energy. It's easy to do. I sit on my feet with my legs bent under me and slowly fold down over my legs. Depending on my need for a shoulder stretch, I may begin by lengthening my arms out in front, then releasing them to the sides of my body, with palms toward the ceiling. Then, centered and aware, I collect my breath and feel what is going on throughout my entire body. It is a fetal position, inward and self-contained. I am a little package. I observe until my mind becomes calm. If that sounds too easy to you, you're right! This has been one of the most difficult asanas for me to relax into for the very reason that it's supposed to be relaxing. It requires a quality of letting go that can be nearly impossible, especially when I need it most.

Letting go and relaxing was something I never let

myself do; it seemed to involve nurturing, like being taken care of by a mother. I had very little experience with that as a child. When I succeed in relaxing these days, I feel as if I am learning to parent myself. I'm learning to give myself the love and care a mother gives her child. My mother had a hard time doing that. The early causes of this failing are lost in the everyday murk of our unhappy family life, but as I neared my teens, things took a much sadder turn. She broke her leg when I was eleven, a severe break, and the doctor sent her to bed for several months with a cast all the way to her hip. Even after she got up, she was very unstable for months more. It seemed to me, as a girl, to be an endless recovery for a broken bone. And then we noticed that she was getting worse instead of better as the weeks went by. She retreated to her room again, and I began my long stint taking care of my mom and our home.

My parents had for years slept in separate rooms on different floors, so I began sleeping in her room. My job was to let the cat in and out, or to help my mother to the bathroom. I loved her desperately, although she was explosively volatile and grumpy, especially in the middle of the night. My dreams were often shattered by a violent kick if I wandered into her space in the bed. No cuddling for us! To this day, I sleep motionless, on my back. She also used the kicking and shoving method to wake me for the cat, or for her trips to the toilet. The worst task was when the cat would throw up from eating a mouse, bones and all; having failed to let the hunter out in time, I had to crouch on the carpet sopping up vomit while my mother moaned in pain and cursed my father for being a no-good son of a bitch who didn't love her or help her, ever. Those were long nights.

I think my plight may have been obvious to neighbors in Sun Valley. Kelly Simpson was my best friend, and her family invited me to go with them on a trip to the beach in California during the spring of my twelfth year. We all drove to the coast in their camper van. I was wonderfully relieved to imagine a few weeks of swimming and sunning and giggling with my friend and her parents; they were so much easier to be around than my own family. Our excitement about reaching the ocean mounted so high that Kelly and I rode on top of the van for the early-morning drive over the final bumpy miles to our parking spot at the beach. I lay on my back, feeling the warm wind and watching the sunrise light the clouds with a pink glow. It seemed I could feel my spirit exhaling after the long months of tension.

I loved the easiness of the beach life. Kelly's parents, Jack and MaryLou, played with us, and never raised their voices unless we giggled too loud in the late-night hours. The days were spent chasing Frisbees, boogie boarding, body surfing, and changing our sandy bikinis. We ended the days listening to ghost stories around a bonfire, pleasantly exhausted from too much sun and swimming. After just four days of this delight, I called home to tell Mom and Dad about the trip, but they weren't there. I was told that they were in Portland, Oregon, and given a number to call. I was amazed that they'd gone off together. My first assumption was that Dad had gone fishing with my godfather and that my mother had somehow miraculously decided to go along to visit my godmother. When I got hold of Dad, though, he told me that Mom was really sick, and it would be best if I was flown to see her right away.

It seemed inconceivable to me that she was sick. She was just recovering from months of being bedridden with her broken leg. In my bafflement, I couldn't think of any questions to ask Dad on the phone, so I was left with a horrible anxiety. *What kind of sickness do they fly you away from your vacation for, and not tell you anything about it?* Dad chartered a small airplane from San Diego, on which I made a long, rough flight up the coast. I spent the hours fighting off nausea and fear, my nose pressed against the cold glass. I picked out points along the route as a distraction from my dread.

At the other end, Dad's dusty green Peugeot was waiting by the airstrip. We hugged, but he was not able to find his voice for several minutes, so we drove in silence. He knew how close I was to Mom, so he found it nearly impossible to tell me that the doctors had found a tumor so big that all attempts to remove it had failed. Simply touching it could spread the malignant cells throughout her body. Cancer had been percolating through her along with the stress and resentment. Her leg was failing to heal because there was an inoperable malignant tumor on her thymus gland. The thymus is the lymph gland at the base of our throats that screens the T-cells of our immune system to make sure they recognize and fight foreign invaders—a nice place for a tumor! The doctors thought her only chance was an intensive regimen of chemotherapy and radiation: brutal with today's technology, and horrific in those days. The likelihood of my mother surviving was not good; they thought she had about two months to live.

Mom during chemotherapy treatments

I grasped the gearshift with one hand and the car door handle with the other, trying to keep the heaving sobs from drowning me. I arrived at the hospital soaked with tears. Dad found me a bathroom where I could get myself in order before going up to Mom's room. I rinsed and rinsed my swollen face because I wanted Mom to see my love, not my fear. She was sleeping when we entered the room, so I stood quietly until she sensed that we had arrived. Looking up, she raised her arms toward me and I rushed into her embrace, failing completely in my resolve to be strong. I begged her to promise that she wouldn't die, and she did. She told me she would never leave me alone.

Eventually, the quiet murmuring of nurses with chores to do made it clear that I had to leave. My exit was backward; I stared at my mother's face, promising her that God and I would not let her die.

Mom came back to Sun Valley for her treatments, and I became the mainstay in her daily care. We would make the three-hour drive to Boise on the days of her radiation and chemotherapy treatments. I enjoyed eating lunch with her, and looked forward to having a club sandwich. She ate too, until she realized it would make her sick later on. While she was in the hospital, I waited in the parking lot or sat on the grass looking for four-leaf clovers. I was always looking for good luck. The drives home were very quiet. She was exhausted and probably shouldn't have been driving, but I was too young to do anything but keep her company.

The nausea would begin after we went to bed. Usually, I was deeply asleep when the sounds of moaning dragged me, disoriented, from my dreams. I would get a wet washcloth and a glass of ice and go to find her wrapped around the base of the toilet, too sick to return to bed and too exhausted to sit up. It was on those nights I learned that silence has a volume. The silence was excruciatingly loud. I longed for somebody to come, or for the cat to need help—anything to break the silence.

I was paralyzed with fear that my mother would die. The bad moments were forgiven. Calling on anything I could think of, I would stand in her room singing like Joey Heatherton advertising Serta Perfect Sleeper mattresses, clowning until she cried with laughter. I lived for that, and she did too. I knew she loved me. Sometimes, she would even let me snuggle up next to her with my head on her chest, just listening to her heart beat, her long, bony fingers gently stroking my head. At those times, I knew I could not bear to lose her. So I began to pray. I prayed day and night, begging God to keep her alive. I sat in the dark in my mother's bed, too afraid to sleep alone in my room now because I believed my prayers and close proximity were needed to keep her from death.

For another six months, we continued our trips to Boise and played out the agonizing nights in the bathroom. She became a wraith, but she survived the treatments. As the effects wore off, it began to seem that she and the doctors had killed the cancer before it killed her. The downhill momentum stopped, and to my hopeful eyes she began to seem a little better.

Margaux, out in California, heard our good reports and arranged to give us relief from the struggle to heal. She had been cast in her first movie and was to play the role of a supermodel who was a victim of rape. The movie also had a part for her character's younger sister. Margaux felt overwhelmed by the challenge of acting, and she thought it would be easier if she worked with me rather than with a stranger. So she suggested to director Lamont Johnson and producer Dino De Laurentiis that I should play the role of her little sister. They flew me to New York for a screen test, in which I was filmed swimming and talking with Margaux. They liked the rapport they saw between us, and the obvious genetic ties were an added bonus. I got the part, and suddenly Mom and I were off on a vacation from our strange life. As the treatments moved farther in the rearview mirror and California got closer in view, she seemed better still. She covered her poor bald head with a scarf and we were finally off. It felt like we had come out of a dark, damp tunnel.

Lipstick was a fascinating experience for all of us. There were several scenes in the movie when Margaux, who was playing a model, was posing in a studio for real-life celebrity photographer Francesco Scavullo. Neither my mother nor I had ever seen Margaux model. She was amazing—she knew how to move her body and make expressions that were sexy and alluring one moment, and then fresh and innocent the next. Margaux came alive in front of the camera. She loved the camera and it loved her. It shocked me. This was nothing like the girl who skipped school, wore baggy painter's pants, and let spit wads fly across the backyard. She was a genuine star and sex symbol. I couldn't figure out where she got all that confidence and sensuality.

Mom and I were impressed and excited, and it got

Lipstick, *with Margaux and Anne Bancroft*

Lipstick

even better because we had a chance to be made up by top professional hairdressers and makeup artists. Mr. Scavullo took my first glamour photos. Just as when he worked with Margaux, he said things like "Darling, beautiful," in his Brooklyn accent. "Gorgeous like that, Beauty. Stay like that, Darling." Wow! I felt like such a success. Of course, after seeing the photos I didn't feel quite like the glamorous, gorgeous darling that Margaux appeared to be, but it was a heady experience for a thirteen-year-old.

The one worry I had during the filming was a scene where I was chased through the innards of the Pacific Design Center by the bad guy, played by Chris Sarandon. For weeks, I begged him not to be too scary when he came after me. I knew it was a movie, but I didn't like the idea of being terrified for any reason. Chris was continually noncommittal; he knew the quality of his own performance depended on scaring me witless. I couldn't separate the movie from reality. Surviving the scene seemed like a matter of real life and death to me.

In the actual event, I needn't have worried. There were so many takes, and so much technical stuff going on, that I truly understood movies aren't real. In the process, I found I could tap into the real experiences of happiness and fear from my past and bring those emotions to the performance. I liked the feeling of excitement that passed through my body when the camera was on me. As long as I'd done my homework—memorized the script and deeply understood the scene—the rest seemed to fall in place when the director yelled "Action!" I felt right acting, letting my emotions out. I loved it!

Throughout the whole experience, my mother was doted on like a queen. She was the mother of a supermodel who was starring in her first film; a model with the clout to get her kid sister a part, too. I hadn't seen Mom so happy in years. From my perspective, my faith in God had pulled her through. I was proud. We had three light and happy months in California.

As soon as we returned to the dark memories of our home in Idaho, the cancer came back. The long struggle that would be her life began again. For a change, Dad drove her to Boise, and that night we had a terribly silent dinner. Afterward, he came to my room and told me that the doctors had found more tumors in her back, near her spine. His words struck me like a physical blow. "Not again. Please, dear God, no more," I begged inside my head. I remember feeling certain that it was a terrible mistake for me to allow myself joy and freedom while making *Lipstick*. My failure to pray obsessively had to be paid for, and the price was my mother's cancer and renewed neediness. Guilt was a hot brand deep in my emotional life, always there to make me believe that joy must be paid for in suffering and hard work. That scar still troubles me as I sit here trying to relax and trying to love myself. If I can get any good out of the experience, it must come from looking at my own daughters and realizing how deep and vulnerable, how precious the thoughts of young people are. Damaged goods are awfully hard to repair. My love for them swells up to fill me.

4

WARRIOR I POSE,
OR *VIRABHADRASANA* I

I am thinking about control today. How hard I have worked to get some feeling of control in my life! Most of the people in my family seemed to be at the mercy of uncontrollable and unhappy forces, so I never wanted to let changes just happen *to* me. I didn't trust life. Clutching hard to make my body and mind do what I thought I wanted, I made myself physically sick and pushed my emotions to the brink of collapse. It wasn't until I began to learn about surrender that I started to change some of my unhealthy patterns. Warrior I pose is a good one for me because it mimics the stance of the great warrior Arjuna as he surrendered his ego and sense of separation from all being, yielding to his fate. That is something I always have to work on.

Warrior begins with a strong stand in Mountain pose.

I'm trying to feel myself truly here, grounded and balanced. Then I take my right foot back into a deep lunge. My left foot remains firmly planted and straight ahead. The shin on that leg is vertical, the thigh parallel to the floor, the knee bent. My right foot is turned out at a forty-five-degree angle and that leg is straight. My hands are raised above my head, straight up from the shoulders or above the head in prayer. My neck is tight today, so I don't look up. Instead, I look out into my lovely garden. This is a powerful asana, but my focus is on avoiding strain. My throat and face are soft and relaxed. I am trying to avoid the tension that will block the flow of energy up my spine. I hold the pose for several minutes, just looking and feeling my solidity. But as the minutes pass, I feel that I'm sinking into myself: my tummy collapses; my back is sinking into my hip. Suddenly I am no longer on top of a posture that is usually very easy for me.

I believe that hatha yoga, like life, is an exercise in passionate curiosity. The mere desire to be curious usually helps me move naturally and inevitably from posture to posture, inspired by nothing more than my body's innate desires. When I am inside my practice like this, I use the moment to observe my body very closely, but also to observe what I *don't know* about myself physically, emotionally, and spiritually. This seems to be the key to creating my own personal practice. Within each posture I satisfy my curiosity by moving my body out of alignment and then back into it. *What feels right?* I always try to remember to challenge my comfort zone because I am likely to be less present and less aware in the easy places. I manipulate my postures into places that are out of my norm, and the feelings teach me a great deal about myself. Sometimes I feel things only physically, but if I stop to imagine my mind deep inside, observing my physicality, I also get emotional insights from those same movements.

Today, in Warrior, I am trying to breathe into my discomfort and collapse to see if I can change the feeling or find a new depth in it. Usually, the pain and mental noise will shift if I look closely and try to figure out where they are coming from. What is this feeling of having the ground shift out from under me? It feels like the times I have gone searching for ways to get out of the pain in my life—pain too often caused by my fear of losing control. I suppose this is what caused me to become obsessed with food and eating when I was about fifteen years old.

Nursing my sick mother, I came to believe that the only way I could avoid the same fate was through controlling what I put into my own mouth. She was a wonderful cook, but as I racked my brain to understand why she was sick, I lit on the idea that it was meat, sugar, and alcohol — especially alcohol—that caused her illness. I still believe that I was partly correct, but I went at it so hard and with so little knowledge that I started a twenty-year roller-coaster ride with my body.

Over the years, I threw myself into diet and exercise programs. At some points I was sure that I was too fat and ugly to get work in Hollywood. I suffered from a vague lack of energy that made me feel as if I constantly had the flu. I tried being a vegetarian, then a vegan, cutting protein and fat out of my life almost completely. My skin went to hell, drying up, cracking, and breaking out just when I had to play close-up scenes in my films. I avoided sugar like the plague, instead eating massive amounts of carbohydrates that promptly turned to sugar in my starved body. Inexplicably still not feeling well, I became a crusader for a macrobiotic diet, shooting dirty looks at my friends and family because I was sure they were killing themselves with their food. My mother returned the sentiment.

Spiraling further out of control, I began to eat only fruit during the day, followed by gorge eating at night. Or I would fast, drinking a succession of iced espressos for a cleansing. I rode the roller-coaster of coffee energy and crashed into letdown and depression, but I was addicted to the feeling of lightness that comes with skipping meals. Eventually, all this metabolic tinkering got me into real physical trouble when my thyroid gland shut down and stopped making thyroxin. Now I truly felt sick and weak on a daily basis.

During this time, my emotional insecurity and my need for some sense of meaning in life caused me to throw myself at a succession of strange spiritual wacks, psychics, astrologers, and holistic doctors. I believed that if I could make them my friends, they would always be there for me with a remedy for my real—and imagined—ailments.

I began this desperate search out of my teenage fears. I was terrified of my mother's illness and the mental instability of my sisters. I had a hard time making the distinction between Mariel as me and Mariel as my mom or my two sisters. The only thing I thought I could control was the way my body looked. And it was clear to me that the females in my family didn't have control of that! I decided

that more determination was what I needed. I associated
fat with losing control, believing that if I became fat it was
a sure sign I was heading toward mental illness. Fatness
was a visual manifestation of losing my grip on reality. I
had no idea of the human comedy, no thought that we are
actors in a great play where we are certainly not writing
the script. I wanted control. And that definitely did not
include softening as God and gravity intend for us to do as
we become women. I got my first period at age sixteen and
it freaked me out. It represented fat to me—fat, moodiness, and lack of control. I willed that I wouldn't let that
happen again, and I held off my second period until I was
twenty-one. After that, I menstruated about twice a year
and was proud because it seemed my amenorrhea was due
to a lack of body fat.

I was lean and mean, like a boy. In not allowing my
female qualities to come fully into bloom, I thought I was
controlling my health and sanity. My female role models
represented nothing I wanted—illness, instability, and
heaviness. Whenever my eldest sister, Muffet, had to be
put on medication, she gained twenty pounds. She was a
beauty and my idol, so it crushed me to see her lose herself. I was determined never to let that happen to me. Margaux had suffered from bulimia since she was fifteen. I
can still remember a family vacation in France when I was
ten and she was seventeen. After meals or in the middle of
the night I could hear her throwing up in the bathroom,
and it terrified me. I was afraid of throwing up from that
time until I had kids of my own to care for. I bought stomach medication to prevent any stomach upset. So, before I
was obsessed with food, I was obsessed with *not throwing up*.

Looking back, I can see that all the things that took over my mind represented loss of control to me.

This personal battle continued in concert with the many hardships my family eventually went through. Every time Margaux would publicly fall into drug and alcohol abuse, I would strengthen my resolve to control my health and my body. When she was released from the Betty Ford Clinic, she was at least fifty pounds overweight, bloated but still speaking out about her recovery. I was devastated. Why would she make a spectacle of herself when she was in that condition? To me, she wouldn't be recovered until she was thin, beautiful, and pulled together again. I was once more identifying too closely with her, which was understandable since people often mistook me for my sister in the eighties and early nineties. They were remembering her modeling days, but I believed people thought I was overweight, too. Did they see something I couldn't see in the mirror? Was I finally losing it myself, and just unaware? Perhaps my family couldn't tell me for fear of throwing me even more off balance. The fear I carried with me became unbearable.

I sought out anybody who could possibly help me get free of my obsessions. It was 1993, and I was newly under the care of Dr. Peter Evans, the holistic chiropractic physician who was to become my trusted doctor and spiritual teacher; still, I was embarrassed to talk to him about my uncontrollable thoughts. Instead, I fell into the care of a so-called spiritual healer. I could reach her only by phone, and she was extremely strict about my calling precisely on time. If I was late at all, she would berate me for not giving her my full energy and attention. I *was* giving her all my money, though. She charged $450 for each call. She had me believing that she was slowly unraveling the great family sickness, going ever deeper into my psyche to kill off the "evil thought forms" that were haunting me. With every achievement, another layer of the onion that was my life was pulled back. Just another $450 check and we could go further into my healing.

This woman had me tied in knots, afraid to leave home for fear I would miss her call. When she finally proposed to meet me, I was so consumed by the thought that I became a stranger to my own family. Nobody understood the amazing work I was undertaking, not only for myself but for them as well. Truthfully, deep inside I was full of doubt, yet I feared this woman's wrath. I had completely given up control; that much is sure. She used whatever psychic abilities she had to pick out my weak spots and keep me needy and off balance. Eventually, she made her way out to Idaho for a visit. I will never forget seeing her. She was hugely overweight and disheveled. Not that it should have mattered, but in my mind the end result of all the work we were doing was to free me of my obsession with food and body fat. I guessed that she was trying to get me to let go and feel OK about it, but that wasn't what I wanted. She must have sensed my terrible discomfort, though I tried desperately to cover it up. She said that she knew I was appalled by her looks, but she was once thin and beautiful. She explained that the sacrifice of her intense work was to take on all the karma and pain of her patients, including me, and that spoiled her looks. Somehow, again, someone else's suffering was my fault.

I began to consider that I needed to get her out of my

life, but her grip on me was strong. To buy some time, I took her on a hike after shuttling the kids off to play with friends. I sadistically planned an eight-mile hike, but we had barely started up the trail when she stopped to show me her talent in alchemy. She told me she would make gold and silver appear in the rocks beside the trail. I actually spent several minutes trying to see the gold she claimed to have created, but she had picked the wrong tactic for avoiding a hike. I had been looking at that same sparkle in the mountain granite all my life. When I realized that she was faking magic because she was in no shape for a hike, my whole fantasy came crumbling down. *What was I doing with this woman?* My eyes were finally open, and my whole being filled with shame.

I got myself home and begged my husband's forgiveness for my bizarre behavior over the past few months. It took me a long time to get over my humiliation and my dip into dopiness. Finally, I forgave myself and began to look at the lessons in the experience. I realized that there is no one pill for healing our pains. Nor does that cure come through magic or psychic miracles. I still consider myself a very spiritual woman, but I believe now that the healing comes through daily meditation and surrender to my highest good, God, and to my teacher. I place my problems at the feet of God and ask for direction.

Instability is learning. The breakdown is the beginning of my understanding. Pain gives me a patient resolve in my faith because it never totally leaves; it just finds different forms. I move through hard and persistent lessons only to make room for new ones. Accepting that such a pattern is all right, I can move fluidly back into balance in my

Warrior pose as many times as I need to, until I get it right. The warrior is reaching to heaven to surrender her ego, to give up the illusion of separation from all being. If I can truly surrender in that way, I might learn to relax my hunger for an illusory control I can never possess.

5

HEAD TO KNEE POSE,
OR *JANU SIRSASANA*

Depending on how fast my body warms up, I do my seated-forward bends either before or after any kind of back-bend postures. Today, I choose to counterbalance my back bend with the bent-leg version of the seated-forward bend. I start by folding my right leg into the top of my left thigh. *Pull that belly in, Mariel!* I flex my left foot, center my hips, and take my arms and eyes up on an inhale. Exhaling, I hinge forward at the waist, releasing down into my left leg and grasping my shin. My shoulders are squared over the left leg and I readjust my hipbones to feel the ground solidly. With several deep breaths, I release into the leg enough to find my ankle— and I begin to giggle. The posture always seems oddly ridiculous and I imagine that I look silly doing it. I feel the pull in my hamstring and in my shoulder. Tightening my center engages muscles all along my spine. I relax my neck and let my shoulders fall from my ears. And with all that going on, I am always tickled by this pose. It's a pleasure to laugh. It releases my tension and breaks down my inability to let go in other postures, and it reminds me of how funny our lives can be.

Today, I remember being called to the phone by my excited mother when I was sixteen. She said, with a gaiety rare in her voice, that Woody Allen was on the phone for me. I had no idea who he was, so I asked her. She said, "Never mind. I'll tell you later. Don't make him wait." So I got on the phone and heard the nasal voice that was soon to become so familiar. He asked if I'd mind coming out to New York to read for him. He had written a part for me in his new fall project—as yet untitled—and I'd have to wait to read it until I met with him. He said he wrote the part after seeing me with Margaux in *Lipstick*. Giggling, I told him, "Sure," and said it sounded like fun. I liked New York.

When I got off the phone, my mother said I had watched his movie *Sleeper* just the week before. I visualized the small, odd-appearing man who seemed to find great pleasure in rubbing an egg. The sexual humor was beyond my virgin comprehension, and I couldn't understand what everybody was laughing about.

So Woody Allen had called, and off we went to the city. A driver met me at the hotel and took me to Woody's offices in Manhattan, where I walked alone and uncertain down a long corridor. Suddenly a small man bustled out of a door and ran right into me. It was the great man himself! He was very sweet and seemed almost as shy as I was.

He made me feel welcome and important and tongue-tied. When I left the office, I was clutching his script like a great mystery. I had no idea what was in it until I got back to my hotel. The scene he wanted me to read shocked me. Half of the sexy stuff was over my head, but I didn't want to admit it. I subtly tried to get my mother to explain things to me, but it was all too embarrassing. In the end, I went back to read for Woody in a dark theater, only partly understanding the racy scene. Most of the time I tried to hide my red face behind the script. I had just graduated from adolescent fart jokes, and here I was talking about sex in front of adults. But the package must have been what he was looking for, because despite my giggles and my soon-to-be-branded "Minnie Mouse" voice, I was shortly making the movie *Manhattan*, in Manhattan, and having the time of my life.

In the mornings, we would shoot scenes in Elaine's and then stay right on through lunch. Elaine doted on Woody in his favorite hangout. When we shot in the art gallery downtown, it was awesome. We were on the streets and in the galleries with the energy of the city around us. Every day at lunch, the cast found another great local place to eat. All the people were wonderful. Diane Keaton was unlike anybody I had ever met; she was so bizarre and so much fun, with her frail body in those great oversize pants and shirts. I remember her sense of style and how much fun she had with herself. That was a big lesson for me. Woody was hard on her in terms of what he wanted out of her as an actress. She was forever reshooting her scenes until he was satisfied. He wanted a quality of pretentiousness that didn't come naturally to her. She never com-

Manhattan, *with Woody Allen*

plained, though. They seemed to understand each other's shorthand from working together on so many projects.

Woody was warm and funny with me. I spent all my free time with him. He took me to museums and his favorite dinner spots. We sat on park benches and invented comical lives that seemed to fit the looks of strangers walking by. Woody constantly made me laugh, and at the same time he treated me as an equal. For the first time in my life, I felt interesting and interested, like an adult. Realizing my complete innocence, he was sharing New York with me in an amazingly generous way.

Obviously, I was far from the sexually astute teenager, Tracy, that I was playing in front of the cameras. There was one traumatic scene where Woody and I were supposed to make out while riding around Central Park in a hansom cab. I was nervous for weeks before the shoot. I'd made out a few times before, but I had no idea whether I really knew how to do it. I practiced on my own arm while looking in the mirror, and asked my mother if she would show me. She rolled her eyes incredulously and said those days were long since over for her. Assuring me it would all be fine, she said they would probably fake it for the film. Yet somehow I knew I was in for a wild ride around the park.

Finally the day came and I was as ready as I was ever going to be. The people in the makeup and hair trailers gave me long encouragement, so that I began to feel I could make it through the scene without fainting. We climbed into the rocking cab—"Action!"—and a couple of dialogue lines later Woody grabbed me like a linebacker making a tackle and kissed me hungrily. It seemed more like the kiss of a schoolboy, but who was I to judge? My lips were pressed tightly together, and oddly, so were Woody's. He instinctively respected my complete terror, and we both managed to get through the park without disgrace. I was drenched with relief. Stepping shakily down to the ground, I asked everybody if it looked all right and they assured me it was fine. I had done it! I had made out on camera! I'd worn a T-shirt and underwear in front of strangers as though I'd had sex. And I'd spoken about scuba-diving equipment as though it were a normal sexual fantasy. I was a veritable adult. The cast and crew made me feel like part of the team.

When the filming ended, I was distraught. I hated the idea of going back to Idaho, where my mother would follow her pattern and soon be sick and depressed again. I couldn't bear it. I wanted the talk about art, music, and Bergman movies to continue. I wanted this film life to go on forever. So I invited Woody to come to Idaho, and he amazed me by saying yes. That was it! In two months he would visit me on my own turf. My parents would be in rare, happy form around a big celebrity. The prospect gave me the courage to go home again, but I lived for Woody's visit.

He arrived in Idaho on a dark November day. It was bitingly cold and Woody said the landscape from the air looked like a moonscape. I think he was about as much at home as he would be on the moon! Barely was he shown to his room than my dad and I dragged him out on a hike through the mountains, with slobbering Labrador dogs at our sides. Of course, we locals couldn't go on a trail, so we bushwhacked straight uphill into a gathering snowstorm. I knew Woody liked exercise—he played tennis several times a week—and he was very fit. It never crossed my mind that he had come straight up from sea level and was gasping for breath in the thin air. Dad was completely in his element, talking jovially about the country. He pointed out all the birds and told Woody what was in season for hunting, which I'm sure was a subject of tremendous interest to him. We Idahoans were oblivious to the deep silence greeting our happy chatter, imagining that Woody was just gazing in amazement at the wildness and power of the storm in the mountains. As we gained altitude, we also gained snow. Each deepening and struggling step made us happier, and made Woody look more waterlogged and exhausted. Fanatics that we were, we had to make it to the top, dogs and all, trailing our miserable guest behind us.

Triumphantly looking out over the valley in the rapidly descending darkness, Dad told Woody about the wonderful dinner awaiting us—a pheasant he had shot just the day before.

So, down we went through the high, snowy sagebrush, guided into the gloom by the lights below, where my mother was slowly and delicately roasting the dead bird with herbs and potatoes. Back at the house, Dad's best Château Margaux warmed the chill out of us. Thank God nobody got any birdshot in the meat. Woody asked Dad if he shot everything we ate. We had salad after the meal, "Like the French do it," my father proudly pointed out, having spent the first eleven years of his life in Paris. My mother ended our meal with a tarte Tatin, the caramelized apples in a dazzling circle covered with fresh whipped cream. I looked fondly at my parents. They were at their best preparing and sharing great food and wine. With a hugely important guest like Woody, they never even spoke a harsh word to each other.

Mom and Dad

Then, as was her custom, my mother headed upstairs to her room to watch television. Dad went down to his quarters in the basement to drink port and eat cheese in front of his TV. Woody stood awkwardly with me in the family room and asked, "It's only eight o'clock. Is that it? We're done for the night?" There was no Elaine's to venture off to for coffee, no Michael's Pub for a good long session with his saxophone. Yes, Woody, that's it. Everybody off to their own rooms, with television or books to take us away from our ordinary, uninspired lives. Clearly, it was not the exciting life I had glimpsed in New York, but it was what I knew, and we had shared the best of it. I never imagined that Woody would go into his room that very night and make arrangements for a private plane to come in the morning to rescue him from his mountain fiasco. I imagine the incident may be in the back of his mind whenever his city characters are horrified by the dullness, the bugs, or the provinciality of country existence.

Taking him to the airport the next morning for his literal and metaphorical flight back to the city, I realized that I was still in the process of figuring out what world I belonged in. I asked him please to stay in contact with me. It was devastating to think of losing the sense of self I had built by spending time with such a totally urbane person. But he dove into his next project, while his producers sent me off to represent *Manhattan* at the Cannes Film Festival. Everybody knew that Woody would never show up at such a scene, so I became the sacrificial lamb. Of course, I was excited to go. It sounded amazing to tour the south of France with my dad, whose first language was French. He could indulge in the great pleasures of food and wine, and

I could see the quaint countryside. My memories of Europe were glowing ones of cobblestone streets, thatched roofs, and walled cities.

Cannes was not the Europe I had experienced before. The white architecture was beautiful against an azure sea, but the place was packed with all kinds of people, united only by the desire to make some kind of breakthrough in films. Desperation filled the ocean breeze. There were seas of young women in bikinis and transparent dresses, literally naked to the world, trying to get a break from any male who pretended to be a producer. It blew my mind, making me think of nothing so much as a freak show.

Most of my time was spent at the elegant Hôtel du Cap, doing one interview after another before being escorted to various outdoor decks, where I was photographed, either alone or with my father. Everyone adored my charismatic, French-speaking dad, finding him to be an irresistible element, and saying so in their articles. I certainly didn't mind—it took the heat off me. The long meal breaks were wonderful. Dad would spirit me away to secluded, charming cafés that served leisurely meals of many courses. I was a bit daunted by the richness of the food, though Dad found it sublime.

The night of the big premiere for *Manhattan* finally came, inducing great excitement among everybody attending the festival. Woody Allen has long been an enormous success in Europe, and the buzz around the film was palpable. I had a gorgeous frock that someone, perhaps Valentino, had given me to wear. I was so out of my depth that I'm not even sure which famous designer dressed me for the night. My preparations in those wonderful days of youth were pretty simple: I scrubbed my face, applying not a drop of makeup; washed and dried my fine, straight hair; then I was ready to go. Dad was dashing in his simple black suit and bow tie, and he was a comforting date for an event that was suddenly beginning to seem like an awfully big deal.

The theater was just a stone's throw from our hotel, but the security people insisted that we be driven in a limo through the impossibly big and dense crowd; we never would have been able to get through on foot. Even in the car, it took forever to inch through the mob to the bottom of the imposing red-carpeted stairway. At either side, ropes held back hordes of photographers, all elbowing and jockeying for position. I exited the car into a wave of sound made up of people screaming my name—"Mariel," "Mariel, here!" "Mariel, over here, *s'il vous plaît.*" Some of the voices sounded friendly, others were demanding, even angry. I tossed my head from side to side, trying hard to please everybody, and becoming increasingly undone as I mounted the seemingly endless staircase. Just before I was rescued by the theater entrance, the edges of my lips began shaking uncontrollably from holding a forced smile. Dad, at my side, was chuckling. "Wow! That was something. Nobody called *you* a sack of potatoes!" It was a relief to hear the old term of endearment he had always used for me, but I couldn't have felt much more like a sack of potatoes than I did at that moment—a lumpy heap of helpless russets.

Ushers seated us in the grand theater just before the movie was announced to great applause. I clutched Dad's hand. I had seen the movie in New York, but this time I felt somehow responsible for it. My heart was beating louder than the sound track's Gershwin coming from the speakers.

Holding tight to my father's hand, I kept telling myself that the feeling would eventually ease up. My eyes were having difficulty focusing and my stomach was in a knot. Every once in a while, the thought would cross my mind that I still had to pass back down that staircase again through

With Scott Glen at the Academy Awards for Manhattan, *while in L.A. filming* Personal Best

the gauntlet of greedy paparazzi, and I could hardly breathe. Halfway through the film, one of the tears rolling down my cheeks fell on my father's hand. He looked at me and understood that I was in trouble. I asked if he thought we could leave right away without going out the front, so he had a quick conference with the security guys. In minutes, they whisked me out a back exit and into a mini ambulance that snaked its way over back roads to the hotel.

Safe inside my room, I ran to the bathroom, where I lay facedown on the cool tile and wept. Dad brought me cold water and told me to get my pajamas on. Always uncomfortable with emotional females, he quickly left me alone to recover. Over the night, I managed to get myself back together for the long flight to Idaho the next morning. Dad patted me on the leg during the ride to the airport and said, "You did OK. It was a lot to handle." It was very true. Fame is a lot to handle for anybody. If you are a kid who believes it is your job to make absolutely everybody else happy, it can be overwhelming. I was awfully glad to see my Sawtooth Mountains smiling their newly melted spring look at me when we flew into Sun Valley.

In a little while, I went on to the grueling filming of *Personal Best*, which felt, in comparison with Cannes, like work I could handle. Woody and I, drawn in different directions, slowly lost track of each other. In some ways, that broke my heart. It was the lesson I had to relearn on every film I have done: you make close friends, create a lovely, important new family, and then you say good-bye. Having come from a family where conversation was either purely surface (What wine shall we have with the trout?) or purely caustic (Are you even going to taste the food before you turn it into a salt mine?), I longed to keep all those perfect film families intact. It never happened.

But I look back with gratitude at how much all those people taught me about life. And one of the best things they taught me was how to laugh, because that was something my own family didn't do well at all. Having that knowledge let me develop one of the nicest aspects of my yoga practice—laughing at myself. Far from being a judgmental competition, yoga can sometimes be a celebration of humor. We are funny beings, and there is a lot to laugh about in ourselves. When doing asanas, the body has some wonderful hidden jokes. Any pose, from the simplest to the most complex, can bring up a ridiculous sense of the giggles, even outright joy. I try to be grateful for anything my practice brings up for me. I am curious about it. Why, of all the possible reactions, did this seated-forward bend make me laugh? It is a constantly unfolding surprise, and accepting that fact is my path to more understanding and joy.

6

CAMEL POSE,

OR *USTRASANA*

Camel pose is an asana that can be per-
formed at very different levels of difficulty. At its simplest,
I stand on my knees and reach behind to grasp my heels;
but in the advanced stages I begin kneeling and bend over
backward until my head is on the floor, cradled by my feet.
Don't try that maneuver until you are really warmed up!
It is an exciting payoff for a lot of work, and it lets me feel
full in my yoga practice.

I go into Camel pose in gentle steps. To begin, I sit in
Virasana with my legs folded and gradually lean back as
though trying to rest my body on the ground. Leaning
back, I put my hands beside my head as I would if I were
going to push up into a full back bend. The push of my
hands connects me firmly to the ground and I concentrate
on the feeling of groundedness. My spine is contracting in

a way I notice clearly before relaxing back down to the floor. Slowly I make my way back up to sit in *Virasana* again. This time, I rise up on my knees, which are hip-width apart. Lifting from my center, I let my hands find my feet and hold on. I play with tightening my butt and releasing it until I can relax completely in my sacrum, butt, and hips, while still visualizing my belly held in.

When I have felt that release, I come back up to standing on my knees again. This is the moment I go into full Camel, bending backward to take my feet into my hands and nestling my head into my feet. Doing it, I feel totally invigorated and confident about myself. In truth, it has always been a show-off pose for me, and though showing off is the antithesis of all yoga instruction, the ease with which I can do the pose and the incredible yogic look of it made it one of the postures that glued me to yoga early on. It was powerful medicine for an insecure young woman to feel credible and accomplished like that. And I badly needed a boost because I was trying to portray champion track athlete Chris Cahill in Robert Towne's movie *Personal Best*. I was a good athlete, but I was not a hurdler or high jumper and definitely not a shot-putter, yet the film required me to look like an Olympic hopeful in those events.

It was the most grueling film I ever made. I began the project as a seventeen-year-old and was twenty when the film was finally released. Months of training and shooting were made longer by a six-month actors' strike. Even after we finished, I had to stay in training for reshoots, of which there were several. These things really do eat up a measurable part of an actress's life. Nine months of training with track coach Patrice Donnelly let me get the *look* of the events down pat. I could appear to be a champion even if the real athletes I ran against had to slow down, or the editors had to fake the height and length of my jumps and throws. In fact, after my critical success in Woody Allen's *Manhattan*, I was beginning to feel like pretty hot stuff. Not only was I getting tons of attention on the track and in the weight room, I was deeply involved in the process of auditioning actresses who wanted to play in a starring role with me. Some of them were famous and some of them later became famous, but all of them had to please me during their readings. I began to think of myself as something special, really for the first time.

I was totally innocent about the film's content. I never felt that I was playing a lesbian, or that it mattered much. To me, Chris seemed young and sexually confused, and I could certainly relate to the young part. Here I was, still a virgin, auditioning actresses who were supposed to play a lesbian love scene with me. I had never yet had to endure an audition in my career, but I had to kiss a lot of girls as they tried for the part. It was funny to me, mostly because it was such a huge deal for them. Some were very timid and embarrassed, and others made a show of sticking their tongues down my throat. Those episodes reminded me of make-out dates gone wrong just months before at the movies in Ketchum. I was still such a kid. And into my young life, like a bad penny returning, came my hopeless family dynamic again.

Margaux visited town and invited me to stay with her in her suite at the Beverly Hilton. I thought it would be nice to spend time with her alone, and it was, in a way. We had a lovely dinner at my favorite health food restaurant. Back at the hotel, she left me watching TV while she went to a meeting at the hotel bar with her agent or manager. She was gone several hours, and I was nearly asleep when she came back up to the room. Immediately, I could tell that she was different. She had a look I'd seen a million times as a kid—the look of somebody who'd had one or two drinks too many. Her smile was pinched and unreal and her sincerity had hostility in it. She asked me to help her rehearse lines and scenes for an audition she had the next day. I swallowed hard, sensing that this was probably not a good idea, but I feared that saying no would piss her off. I proceeded to read the lines with her, feeling deeply uncomfortable that her dialogue sounded so off-key in my ears. I remember trying to explain that she should think of her character just like herself, only with a different name and life—that she shouldn't think about acting, but speak the same way she was talking to me between scenes. We did it over and over, but she never understood. The more she wanted to go on with it, the more I knew we should stop. I was a poor teacher and she couldn't get it. I wanted so badly to go back across town to my little apartment.

Finally, she gave up without even knowing the lines, deciding she needed to sleep. The lights went out and I lay relieved and cautious in my bed next to hers. Soon, I heard the heavy breaths of a person passed out rather than asleep. I could hear my heartbeat returning to normal in my chest. Eventually the emotions of the odd night subsided, allowing me to slip off into deep sleep.

I was awakened by the sensation of hands gripping my throat. I thought I might still be dreaming—one of those nightmares where I feel like I'm being held down, only nobody is there, and I can't move, I can't scream. Then I heard Margaux's most bitter voice saying, "You think you're so great. You think you know it all, but you're not the big sister, you know." I knew then I wasn't dreaming, but I'm quite sure Margaux was. I dug my fingernails into her hands to make her let me go and she crawled back to her own bed, dumbfounded, with no idea why I'd attacked her. I felt that her subconscious was lashing out at me—in truth, lashing out at herself. These were the heaviest of her drinking and drugging days. Her acting dreams, which she'd had since she was little, had never worked out. The critics were unkind. Then along came her little sister, with accolades and opportunities at my fingertips, as it seemed, right from the beginning.

Needless to say, I didn't sleep the rest of the night. I even left the false safety of the bed, to stand by the window looking out over the lights of Los Angeles. It was a bright, busy place. I think it was the first time I had ever watched the night leave and the day arrive, and I was tired in the morning. Margaux was kind again and very loving. She was eager for her audition. I wished her well and told her to do great. I remember praying that she would. She never called to say whether she got the part, but I learned from my dad, to whom she told everything, that they turned her down. Margaux and I were careful with each other for years after, only slowly building up trust in each other.

I was young and upset, something I need to remember when I start to get down on myself for what happened next during the filming. The power I seemed to have over decisions on the set gradually intoxicated me. I was living the part of a star, and then Robert Towne cast a young woman in the role opposite me who was a wonderful actress but a less than believable athlete. Initially, I felt sorry for her terrible struggles to run like a real sprinter. She was a city girl who was really unaware of her physicality. Somehow, the process of imitating a runner never got easier for her and she was eventually let go from the movie. And no sooner was she on a plane out of there than Robert cast his athletic consultant and lover, Patrice Donnelly, in the role. She was the former pentathlon star who had been training me, and I suspected that she was his choice all along. She was a beautiful athlete but not an actress. I had often been annoyed with her during training. She was very controlling of me—too much like a director, I thought. Also, I was sure she wanted the part. Looking back, I realize that I was projecting my insecure anxiety onto her, but I had no way of knowing that.

I became irrationally infuriated. Clearly, I was out of the inner loop now, even though I was an acclaimed actress and a proficient athlete. Probably "surly brat" would be a good way to describe me. I couldn't get enough people to bad-mouth Patrice and join me in my disgust over her relationship with *my* director. I managed to become incredulous at her lack of acting talent every single day. It was beyond me to admit that Robert, through strange all-night emotional bouts with Patrice, was coaxing a beautiful performance out of her. I could no more admit to her being good in any sense than I could claim I came from a healthy family. Day after day I went out of my way to make her look bad, without realizing that

Personal Best

along the way, I had turned into the unprofessional little prima donna.

One hot summer day on a track near Santa Monica, Robert came over to where I was warming up while waiting for a shot to be arranged. "Stretch," he said, "I want to talk to you." We went into my trailer, where he proceeded to tell me what a pain in the ass I had become. He said that I was actually performing less well than he had hoped, and that my efforts to make Patrice look bad were backfiring. I was the one who needed help—I was the failure. I can still vividly recall the flood of shamed tears draining out of my body. Since I had first acted in *Lipstick*, I had prayed that I would never lose myself, becoming stuck-up or, worst of all, inconsiderate of others.

There I sat in my big, stuffy star trailer realizing that I had become everything I had feared. Colorless and shaken, I sobbed uncontrollably for hours. I must have held up production for a long time. I was a show-off gone wrong, and it felt like the worst possible waste of all I had been given. Finally I got off my bed, washed up, got the red out of my eyes, and let the makeup artist put ice on my face. Self-conscious for days after, I never made myself a problem on a set again if I could help it.

So, today, in my exotic Camel pose, I concentrate on feeling the intense humility of life and all its lessons. Bent in this extraordinary posture, I am challenging my spine and breath and centeredness. I am searching to find the true depth of my gratitude for being able to live and move in this amazing life. Our beauty hasn't got much to do with how we look on the outside—it arises from our inner peace.

7

DANCER'S POSE,
OR *NATARAJASANA*

Dancer's pose is a beautiful pose with tremendous power. The arms and raised leg form a human bow that has the same balance and contained tension that an archery bow has. As with any advanced moves, I do it only after warming up thoroughly with Sun Salutations and deep yogic breathing. When I'm ready, I stand in Mountain pose, feeling my connection to the earth. The toes of my left foot spread and I engage all the muscles in that leg, while bending my right leg up behind me. Opening my right palm to the side, I reach back and take my raised foot in my hand, thumb cradling the arch and fingers holding the inside of my ankle and the top of my foot. My left arm extends to the sky as I begin to concentrate on pushing my right foot back into my hand. The push slowly extends my body and compresses my spine into a back bend. My hips are straight and forward, and looking ahead into the mirror, I can see my foot rising up behind my head. It feels elegant and dynamic. At this moment, I imagine myself as a Greek goddess in a white tunic with golden arm and leg bands.

OK...the image of the goddess fades into a snow-filled screen when I start to lose my balance. It is a very difficult pose to hold. I am reminding my stomach to be pulled in and keeping my hips level and my arm up; and don't forget to keep that foot pressing into the hand! With all that going on in my head, my balance is tenuous at best. Some days I can get it all together by deeply focusing on a fixed point ahead of me. Other days, like today, I have to give it several patient tries, first to the right, then left, then right again until I find my balance. It is worth the effort since beautiful, dynamic postures like this make me feel alive. They also quietly challenge my sense of self, and that is something I have always been willing to struggle with.

Claiming my identity as a woman was a difficult task for me. I was always attracted to tough physical challenges as a girl, usually trying to show the boys in Sun Valley that I could climb or ski better than they could. I'm afraid, though, perhaps as a result, that they admired me more as a pal than as a girl. It probably did not help that I went through my teens tall, lanky, and undeveloped—a girl nobody noticed as a girl. Then came *Personal Best*, with all the macho athletic training and lesbian scenes. That movie seemed to push me to the end of my rope on the androgynous roles. After that, I was determined to make career choices that highlighted me as a woman. But before there were to be any more movies, I wanted to do something fun and free.

Ever since I'd made *Lipstick,* my money had been saved in a trust that I couldn't touch until I was eighteen. I'd supported myself in New York by cleaning people's apartments and walking dogs, and I had always dreamed of owning land and building my own house in the mountains. Now that I was old enough to get the money, it was burning a hole in my pocket. I'd sketched out my dream cabin in the film-script binder while making *Personal Best.* For inspiration, I had the example of my close friend Thekla Von Hagka, who had built a log cabin on the Big Wood River near Sun Valley. I was thrilled and astonished that this young woman had done a huge amount of the work on her own home. When *Personal Best* wrapped up, I headed to Idaho looking for the mountain scene in my imagination, ready to do the same thing.

Dad helped me look for land around Sun Valley, but it didn't take very long to learn that everything in the

With Margaux at one of her weddings

fashionable resort area was priced way beyond my means. Fortunately, Dad had discovered most of the beautiful places in the northern Rockies during his innumerable fishing trips. He knew practically every mile of the Idaho landscape, so we loaded the dogs into the car and searched for more affordable acreage down along the Salmon River. On our first outing, we found twenty acres about twenty miles outside of the little town of Salmon. The place looked like my fantasy: it was a gorgeous little valley filled with green meadows and lush fruit trees, cut by the meanders of Fourth of July Creek.

I wanted it. I could afford it. Dad seemed incredibly pleased with the prospect. We walked the land and discussed its possibilities, noting how the lower elevation allowed a longer growing season and more productive agriculture than we were used to in Sun Valley. It crossed my mind that the critters might be different, too. I asked Dad if he thought there might be rattlesnakes on the land, to which he replied, "Oh, yeah. You're going to come across some rattlers on occasion." This was a scary thought for me. I hated rattlesnakes. The thought of stepping on one lying hidden in the grass made my palms sweat. And of course, having invited the idea in, we immediately came across an enormous rattlesnake shedding his skin. My voice came out as a choked whisper. "Dad, look, there's one right here."

"Yeah," he replied, "kill it."

I paused, frozen in place, really, looking at the snake, which was ignoring us.

"How, Dad?"

In reply, he simply bent down, picked up a boulder, and handed it to me. I shuffled over carefully, as close to my victim as I dared, and let the boulder fall from my shaking hands. Splat! Snake mush. I was amazed by two things: how easily I'd killed it, and how matter-of-fact Dad had been about the whole business. This house-building project, it seemed then, was going to require some new emotional attitudes on my part. During the entire process of building the cabin, though, I never again encountered another snake as big or as close as that one. All the activity must have scared them off into the hills.

We bustled back to Sun Valley to organize. Thekla introduced me to a couple of young guys eager to help me build my cabin. The log house they had built for themselves was beautiful, so I hired them and two of their friends. We all headed back up north to Salmon in the spring of 1980, eager for an early start on the construction season. It was still cold and wet, so the first order of business was the construction of shelters. I'd bought a tepee from a retiring

My four hunks

hippie, and the boys had another tepee and several white canvas tents. It took us a good two weeks to set up camp. We put board floors in all the tents and both tepees. I hung quilts over my bed and others from the side poles, closing off spaces for clothes and toiletries. With a tape deck and dog bed, I completed my cozy retreat. Outside, we set up a kitchen half covered by a canvas tarp to keep the food dry. We installed a generator to run a small fridge and a light. The fire pit was close by. The boys built a table and benches, which I provided with daily flowers and fruit. Altogether, our campsite looked like something straight out of the old West. It was to be the scene of one of the most delightful summers of my life.

I played wife and boss to four gorgeous young men, nursing crushes on all of them. Especially Charlie! He was the oldest, the main decision guy, and he was my fantasy of the perfect husband. He was big and burly and tireless and, best of all, happy and optimistic at every turn. I could easily imagine him moving into my log dream home with me, able to fix any problem and happy to run out to hunt and fish for our winter supplies. He would enthusiastically attack any predator who threatened us. Charlie filled my head with such thoughts of comfort and protection! On the other hand, Todd, mountain climber, mega outdoor man, was the material lust is made from. His Nordic good looks included perfectly mapped-out abdomen muscles that flared into broad shoulders, all topped by a frighteningly sweet smile in a blue-eyed face.

One evening, after we had finished building the sub-floor, we decided to celebrate by cranking up some reggae music and dancing all over the newly created surface. I wore my bikini and the boys had nothing on but shorts. Most of them were not skilled dancers, but Todd had moves that Swedish boys shouldn't know about. I have always loved dancing and believe I can turn on some serious sex appeal when I get into it, so it wasn't long before Todd and I squared off as a couple. The others were hooting and hollering encouragement to us as we danced more and more outrageously. If the others hadn't been there to chaperone us, I probably would have been in trouble that night. The lustful tension between us lingered for weeks afterward. If I happened to brush against him while we framed up the cabin, I felt such a rush of passion that I would have to run off to the store for our daily food, or find some other errand to take me away.

I was puzzled all that summer by the fact that none of the boys ever made a pass at me despite my obvious interest. It was surely not my idea! Charlie, who has remained a friend, recently confided in me that he told each of the boys that they would be looking for another job if he caught them messing around with the boss lady. Bummer!

My days were filled with the chores of the kitchen and being the gofer on the construction site. I did the trips, twenty miles in to Salmon for supplies, and worked on every aspect of cabin building except the finish work. (My hammer work had a tendency to leave big smile marks around the nails.) When the logs arrived, the crew assembled them into a cabin shape in just one day. It was amazing to see it go from just a thought to an actual cabin, even without a roof. My house was becoming a reality!

Most days after the food run and before dinner, I ran for miles up the service road into the hills, thinking about

The cabin under way

my house, my boys, and the feeling that this was the first time I'd felt so free in my life: no mom to care for, no movie-set schedule. I was doing all I wanted to do in the ease of summer. Dad built me a little spring-fed pond on the property and, of course, stocked it with brown trout. We began a morning tradition of jumping into the cold, cold water. It was a contest to see who could get in first and earliest. I felt I had to put on my bathing suit, while the boys—damn their torture of me!—were always naked. We never missed a day except for the few weekends the guys left to go to Wallace, Idaho. I eventually found out that they were visiting a whorehouse there. Wow! If they had realized how much I adored them, maybe they wouldn't have had to make the trip.

On those lonely weekends I had only the company of my yellow Lab, Stitch. I would read by a tiny light and fall into sleep that was usually interrupted by the sound of a bear rummaging in the kitchen for food. They loved cantaloupes especially, and would break open the honey and jam jars in a general destruction of the whole place. Stitch barked frantically from the safety of the tepee. I awoke in the morning, groggy, having to face the huge mess the bears had left in the kitchen. I looked forward to having the guys return, so I could feel needed for constructive activities again.

Too soon, fall weather arrived, sending us to Salmon or a nearby café for dinner in the cold evenings. Our routines were winding down, but we still began each day by diving into the now icy pond. Finally came a day in late November, after my nineteenth birthday, when the house was basically finished. I was doing some last minute chinking between the logs while the boys sanded and stained the woodwork. The appliances were in, and I now did everybody's laundry in my very own washer and dryer. The day I knew was going to be the final day dawned very cold. It was way below freezing. I could hear Charlie outside building the fire, probably sure that we were done with the morning swim. I poked my head outside, said, "Good morning," and watched my words hang frozen in a foggy cloud. Seized by a wild impulse, I put on my frosty bikini, grabbed my towel, and ran hollering down to the pond. To the boys' wonder and consternation, I broke the ice with a stick and jumped right in, wordlessly daring them to follow. Trapped, they all stripped down and ran to join me in the near-death experience. The exhilaration that followed the total body clench of hitting the water was wonderful. We laughed crazily at our madness! They all patted me on the back like the buddy I had become. I was sobered by the thought that all our camaraderie was about to end, but buoyed by the fact that I had organized and helped build a house just for me.

With the house done, I needed to get back to acting again to revive my bank account, and I was sure I wanted a role that featured me as a woman. I thought I'd found the perfect part when I learned of Bob Fosse's project *Star 80*. It is the true story of Dorothy Stratten, a beautiful *Playboy* playmate who was shot and killed by her husband. I believed I understood Dorothy's vulnerability and need to be loved, and I wanted to explore what she projected so powerfully—the sexy, womanly side of my own personality. So my agent, Sam Cohn, who also worked with Bob, proposed that I play the lead in the film. Bob was instantly against the idea of casting the athletic, prepubescent lesbian from *Personal Best* in his movie. I was stunned. It was the first time I had ever been turned down for a part, and my relentless letter-writing campaign didn't change his mind. He told me that he was impressed by my tenacity, but he simply could not see me playing a voluptuous sex symbol.

I knew I had to play this role to free myself from my lifelong tomboy stigma, but it wasn't easy convincing Bob Fosse. I was living in the log cabin I built myself in the wilds, so everything about my home and life testified to my masculine independence. The situation called for drastic action. I decided to go to New York and get breast implants—as if a chest could stand in for a lifetime of experience about being feminine! I was just nineteen, too young to be making such an important decision, but my parents had no say in my life, since I'd been living on my own for three years already. So I got on a plane back to my favorite city and began looking for a plastic surgeon.

In no time, I was sitting in the imposing office of a well-respected and conservative surgeon, telling him of my determination to augment my chest so I could look like a woman, feel like a woman, and defy the genetics of my family. He told me not to do it. He said that I was very young and perhaps nature would fill me out if I would just wait a few years. It made me love him. He was so fatherly and concerned; I just knew he was the one I wanted to perform this oh-so-important-for-my-life procedure. Being the convincing girl I was at the time, I finally got him to agree to do it, especially since I had requested custom-made implants in size extra small. No huge boobs for me—I just wanted to look feminine.

I went into surgery with no trepidation, feeling delirious with excitement. Awakening in pain later, I still managed to stumble to the mirror to check out my new prizes. The wait for the bandages to come off seemed to last forever. When I finally got to examine my coming-of-age implants, I was ecstatic. My instinct was to show them to all my friends, and for several months I did just that. Every time I met a friend, I immediately pulled them aside to lift up my shirt and show them my new look. My breasts really didn't feel like part of my body yet, so it seemed natural to share my joy and see how people reacted. It took months before my breasts began to seem like a private part of me, a part not meant for public display.

When I was sure that I looked normal, I set out after Bob Fosse again. My body was no longer a problem, but I was still not an easy sell as Dorothy Stratten. Mr. Fosse made me audition for him at least half a dozen times. I pleaded that I understood Dorothy's personality, having spent so much of my own life trying to please others. That trait was exaggerated to a desperate degree in Dorothy, and it eventually played a role in her husband's murderous onslaught. As I read again and again, Fosse seemed to make his decision to give me the role. In the later readings there was a shift, so that Bob was no longer auditioning me but examining his script. He wasn't about to tell me I had the part, though, until he was certain his story was making sense. When he finally told me I was the right woman for the role, I was completely thrilled. Fosse cast Eric Roberts in the costarring role, completing preparations.

We began a process of filmmaking unlike anything I had yet encountered. For six weeks, we rehearsed as though it were a play. All the sets were taped out on a stage floor, and by the fifth week Fosse was timing the movie as we went from scene to scene. By the time we shifted production to Los Angeles, I was spending a lot of social time with my director. His mind was fascinating to me as he worked ever deeper into the film. He wanted me saturated with Dorothy's images in print and on film so I could learn her mannerisms and, basically, learn a little more femininity. Fosse taught me how to walk in high heels, which made me wonder how he knew. He choreographed all my photo sessions as though they were stage dances. It was infinitely exciting to me. I was claiming part of my power as a woman, a part I had really known nothing about. And if I'd had any more experience I would have known what was coming.

One night after dinner at the Beverly Hills Hotel he began really flirting with me. All my instincts crashed

Playing Dorothy Stratten in a Star 80 *glamour shot*

together inside. I adored him. I desperately wanted him to like me and be attracted to me, partly because I doubted that anybody *could* like me. I didn't like myself very much. But I was not at all ready for a relationship with him. All the experimenting I had been doing with my femininity had been coming out as sexual energy without my knowing it consciously. My fear and discomfort were overwhelming. I squirmed and tried to make light of his advances as we returned to my hotel room. Closing the door, he practically chased me around the couch until, heart pounding, I pulled myself together and demanded that he please stop. At first he called me a cock tease, which hurt because I wasn't really sure what he meant. He then told me, "I've never *not* slept with my leading lady!" In shock, and expecting to be dismissed from the film, I said, in a high and cowardly voice, "Well, meet the first!"

I managed to collect my excruciatingly high voice, one that he teased me about later, and explained that I didn't feel that I could be naked on the set of his movie all day, playing a *Playboy* centerfold in a deeply dramatic role, and then come home at night and be naked with him. I told him I felt that I would have no soul left. I needed time that was my own, to gather my sense of *me*, before I could return to the victimized role of Dorothy. Being so new to female feelings, I needed time to allow myself to be OK with showing my nakedness daily to every stranger on the set. It was no longer a matter of showing my new breast implants to my friends—this went much deeper than that. I will always be grateful that Bob Fosse honored my request from that day on. I think he may even have respected me for it.

He probably also used our little tussle to shape my performance. Periodically he would come up to me on the set and tease me about my horribly high voice, my coltish legs, or my freeway-wide face. I sensed that the criticisms came from my rejection of him. On those days, I walked the fine line of making myself appealing to him, so he would like me, without implying that I wanted to have sex with him. It was not an easy feat. My feminine confidence was still not intact and it seemed critical to my survival that I be loved. So, we rode a roller-coaster. Some days Bob Fosse saw me as beautiful and sexy, poised and dynamic, and I loved the work. Other days he seemed to look at me with disgust, derailing my focus completely, leaving me needy and insecure. And now, I see that both versions of me were needed to fully capture Dorothy Stratten.

I knew how to play her because I knew this struggle too. I had experienced deep feelings of beauty, and then known the fall into insecurity and confusion. I really had to learn to feel like a woman. When I did, I realized how wonderful that can be, but those wonderful feelings have always been fragile for me. I can easily be knocked back into doubting myself. The big difference for me now is that I have learned that I can fall down from a place of beauty and then pick myself up, uninjured, to experience my beauty again.

The full story of my breast implants is an odd twist on this theme. I eventually came to mistrust the false, augmented beauty the implants gave me. Probably this line of thinking started while I was nursing my first daughter. I was keenly aware of the contradiction of being such a health-conscious person yet having silicone in my breasts. I wondered, too, if the silicone was interfering with my milk production or the flow of milk to my baby; she breast-fed incessantly, and I worried that she wasn't getting enough milk. My breasts were certainly big enough; silicone plus lactation equals extremely large and embarrassing boobs. I had loved the busty look for only about a year before I became self-conscious and began wearing big shirts most of the time to cover myself. Far from building confidence, my womanly look had turned into something I wanted to hide. I felt like a bit of a freak—as though I wasn't being honest about myself.

By the time I turned thirty, all these misgivings gained momentum when my breasts began to feel unusually hard. The implants had always been firm, of course, and I'd never really had breasts of my own to compare; but I decided that I ought to have them looked at by a doctor. The doctor determined that the implants had ruptured, and he planned surgery to remove them. I was worried that the operation would leave me looking deformed, so I asked the surgeon to put in small saline implants so I would still have some shape. The surgery was a difficult job; the silicone had to be scraped out of my breast cavity before the new implants were inserted. There was silicone sailing around all through my bloodstream.

I was very worried about the new medical findings that silicone could cause harm to the immune system. Feelings of immortality do not run rampant in *my* family! So when I learned of a procedure that could turn silicone into silicone citrate, which the body can flush out, I decided to try it. The procedure involved spending ten hours in a small chamber pressurized with hyperbaric levels of oxygen. It was incredibly claustrophobic for me; I could only endure it for two hours at a time, so the treatment went on for five days. My meditation techniques were then pretty basic, so the two-hour stretch was an ordeal survivable only by watching videos on a tiny screen at the foot of the bed where I lay prostrate. If the movie was at all disturbing, I found I could feel and hear my blood rushing through my veins.

Five days could hardly go by more slowly than those did! At the end, though, microscopic examination of my blood showed that the silicone crystals were much fewer and smaller and therefore likely to flush out in my urine and sweat. I was so relieved that the procedure seemed to have achieved positive results.

Before long, I was worrying about the saline implants. I hated having foreign objects in my body, and even these harmless pouches of salt water were encased in silicone plastic. It felt so wrong to me that I finally decided to remove them for good, regardless of the misshapen sacks I was likely to end up with. It seemed a small price to pay to get back the body God had intended for me to have. Feeling that way before the surgery, I was tremendously delighted when my breasts regained a very normal shape and size rather quickly after the implants were removed. I believe my yoga and hiking helped with the speedy recovery. I could not have been happier—I liked what I was supposed to look like! It seemed that I had developed a nice, feminine shape anyway. Had I not gotten implants at age nineteen, I would have seen myself naturally become the female I longed to become. I'm glad to have reclaimed myself—nothing fake and nothing inside to cause an unhealthy surprise in the future.

Standing Bow pose gives me a clear reminder of this waxing and waning of beauty. Real beauty does not come from the full dynamics of a complex posture, just as it does not come from great bone structure, silicone, or the accolades of playing a marvelous role in a movie. Real beauty comes in taking meaningful action in our lives. The present moment of action and observance is where I find my joy and my peace.

8

BRIDGE POSE,
OR *SETU BANDHASANA*

I go into advanced poses like Bridge only after I have done my usual warm-up in the various standing postures that seem like the basic schoolwork of my practice. Mountain, Triangle, Warrior, and a few other poses have taught me the basics of yoga, and they continue to instruct me today. In them, I feel the strong connection between the earth and my feet, and that gives me a focused intent. The energy flows from the earth into the base at my feet and up through my spine to open my heart. My breath spreads the warm current throughout my whole system before it flows out of my hands. This is the simple basis that gives rise to more and more complicated insights, just as the lessons of elementary school lead to those of junior high and so on through more advanced studies. I learn more at each graduation until finally being unleashed into the world on my own.

Bridge pose seems to form a link between the basic understanding and the deeper insights of more intense poses. To go into it, I lie on my back with my legs bent and my knees a little apart, my arms by my side. I put pressure into my feet, always wanting to be reassured by that contact. Slowly, I raise my spine from my coccyx all the way to my neck. I try to feel each vertebra as it releases from the floor. When I am arched as high as I can go, I gather my arms beneath my back and clasp hands with my fingers interlaced. This Bridge is considered a moderate pose, but I do it slowly and intently, focusing on increasing the arch by raising both front and back and pressing my shoulders and forearms down. My heels are pushed into the floor to stretch my legs. Doing it this way, I feel a surge of energy and blood. Peace fills me as I hold and release the posture a few times. It is a transitional posture, the beginning of deeper, more powerful back-bend poses.

I have always been acutely aware of the transitional moments in my life. I have already described the vaporization of my childhood at the moment I learned that Mother had cancer; from then on, I was a confused teenager feeling like a kid and being treated like an adult. Thankfully, the events that mark what I consider to be my entry into adulthood were a lot more pleasant. I was twenty-three years old, living alone on the Upper West Side of Manhattan. Much of my alone time in those days was spent dreaming of the day I would fall in love. Across the street lived a good friend whom I'd met on a theater project. Richard Lombard was my confidant, my no-sex boyfriend. We spent hours together at films and in restaurants, discussing our futures, and we had developed a fairly elaborate schedule of dates. May 11, 1984, was midtown-movie night. As we made our plans, he suggested that we had to go to the new Hard Rock Café just to say we had been there. It was not the kind of place that appealed to me—loud, crowded, and too cool for its own good. Richard was insistent, though, and pointed out that *Dangerous Liaisons* was playing just across the street. Finally, I gave in and we launched ourselves into the crowd in Central Park. When we'd come out the other side of the park, it wasn't too hard to find the hot spot, because it was at the end of one of the longest queues I'd ever seen, longer than at any movie premiere I'd been to. It was totally daunting. I turned to Richard and said, "I'm outta here."

Burly bouncers out front were selecting appropriately cool types from the crowd and making neat little paths for the occasional celebrities who were dashing in from large black limos. I was spotted as I tried to get my friend to leave. Vincent D'Onofrio, the now incredibly accomplished actor, was the bouncer who shepherded me in. He was to let me in most nights for months after that until he left the café to concentrate on his film career.

The noise inside was huge. We were swept up the stairs to the roped-off section, where only the coolest of the cool were allowed. Admittedly, it was a place like no other I had seen, filled with impressive rock and roll memorabilia, like Elvis's white beaded jacket and one of Keith Richards's favorite guitars. Amazingly loud music gave cover to the purposeful staff working to make sure the customers ate, drank, got merry, and moved on quickly so that others could fill their tables. It was an impressive operation.

In spite of the fact that I had to scream for Richard to even hear me, we were soon deep in a conversation about our favorite topic—falling in love. I was sure that I would never fall in love again, sure that my childhood romance with Sean Petersen from the ages of six to fourteen would remain the pinnacle of my emotional life. As I sat faced with this desolation, a clear plan emerged in my head and I heard myself shouting that I would have a baby in a year or two, after I had spent some time living in Paris, on the Left Bank, where my grandfather had lived in his early twenties. It was seeming like a more perfect idea with each passing moment in the giddy atmosphere. I'd find a pied-à-terre, wear all black, smoke Gitanes, and become an incredibly interesting actress in both Europe and the States. Then I would have my baby, sans papa, and raise her as a French girl in Paris.

My mind circled back to the sad fact that I would never fall in love again. There were so few men in New York I was attracted to. I needed a man who seemed as if he had lived outdoors—a cowboy, yet with the intellect and street savvy of somebody verging on urban decadence. He had to be good-looking, rugged, sexy—OK, he was the Marlboro Man with city smarts. As I was saying this to Richard, I looked to the stairs and saw a young man in well-worn Levi 501s, rough-out boots, and a warm blue denim shirt rolled at the sleeves. He had a head full of thick strawberry blond hair down to his shoulders. His jaw was strong and his nose was slightly broken and he was wearing dark sunglasses in the dark restaurant. I pointed him out to Richard, saying, "See that guy coming up the stairs? That's the guy I want to marry."

We both watched dream dude ascend the stairs and pass our table, by which time I couldn't stand it anymore. He looked even better up close. "Oh, please, let's hurry up and leave. I'm depressed now. Guys like him are either gay or already married." But the check took its time arriving, which gave my guy two or three more chances to walk by our table. I could never tell if he even saw us, disguised there behind his nefarious shades. Oh well, I thought, let's see our movie. The Paris plan will begin soon enough— which goes to show what a gifted psychic I am!

The very next night, my girlfriend Liz Houghton asked me to rendezvous with her at the Hard Rock Café before moving on to a party at one of the happening clubs, like Zenon. I groaned and told her I couldn't face the place again. "I was there last night. It's loud and crowded and I hate being picked out of the crowd while everybody else stares daggers at me for jumping the line. It reminds me of the lost Studio 54 days." She begged me to come just for a minute. She had to meet a blind date there and then we would move on to the party. I caved in, but arranged some sort of emotional protection by calling my friend John Goodman and asking him to meet me at the restaurant. We had just finished doing a play together in Dallas, Texas, and the thought of having him along was comforting. So I found myself heading off through the park again, arriving early at the same packed scene outside the café. Worried that the bouncers might not let John inside, I found Vincent again and told him about the bigger-than-life friend who would soon arrive.

Inside, I was immediately escorted upstairs to the cool section and left to stare impatiently at the rock memorabilia as though I actually cared about it. After a few minutes, my blank wandering was arrested by the reappearance of the cowboy. He was dressed as before, except that the denim had been replaced by a Mediterranean blue button-up shirt. And tonight he had lost the dark glasses! I felt a thrill of adrenaline as he came straight across the room toward me—yes, he is coming to see me! He introduced himself and asked who I was, but I was distracted, gazing into his deep brown and elusive eyes. Apparently, my subconscious had been busy without me, because in just twenty-four hours I had developed a huge need to talk with this man, be near him, and share everything. Within minutes that seemed like hours and hours that felt like seconds, I knew so much about the way he thought about life. He shared his dreams of making documentary films, of writing, of returning to explore more of India. My sharing felt inadequate. I thought my life in Idaho and my acting would seem inconsequential to someone with such an accomplished past and brave future. Yet, he *did* seem interested . . .

At some point in our conversation, my friend Liz managed to penetrate the private fog that had surrounded us. She had arrived, met her blind date, and wanted us to get out of there. Sensing that I wasn't at all present with her, she insisted that I join her in the bathroom. I agreed, dimly realizing that I could find out if she knew this amazing man I'd met. "Do you know that guy I was just talking to?"

"I didn't really notice him. What's his name?"

"Steve Crisman."

"Oh, Steve. Yeah. I know he's all right. He manages this place."

That's the magic of love. Here was my friend giving this

flat appraisal while I was so smitten I felt as though I were immersed in water. Sounds were strange and muffled and things felt slowed down. I no longer heard Liz's concerns about her date that evening. My whole energy was focused on the need to get back to the table with Stephen. (I quickly learned that he wasn't fond of being called Steve.) Tearing away awkwardly, I dove through the crowd toward our table, hoping to re-create the little bubble of oblivion we had shared. I was dismayed when Stephen told me he had to leave for a business meeting. It was ten-thirty at night! I chalked it up to running a bar and began praying that he would come back. He paused, turning to me, and said he would return in thirty-six minutes and eighteen seconds— my first experience of a Crismanism I have lived with for eighteen years since. And indeed, in thirty-six or so minutes he did return.

With his departure, the scene in the bar came rushing back to my senses. John Goodman had arrived and was making a boisterous scene trying to let me know he was trapped downstairs. My radar had been focused so completely on falling in love that I had forgotten that I had a date for the evening. Oops! I'm sure John was getting a bit toasted and impatient, but I was afraid that if I went downstairs to see him I would miss Stephen when he came back. I'm ashamed to say that I just let the situation sort itself out. Years later, John and I did the *Roseanne* show together and I thought about that night, but he was very sweet and didn't mention it.

Stephen eventually came back to me through the crowd. We continued our quest to discover anything and everything about each other. By two-thirty the downstairs was

quieting down and everybody I knew was long gone, totally
unnoticed by me. Stephen asked if he could walk me home
through Central Park. I agreed, somehow feeling no qualms
about doing something that I never would have considered
on an ordinary night. I may have been from Idaho, but I
knew there were things you didn't do in the big city—like
walk late at night through the park. But on that night my
feelings of comfort and security were so apparent that I
felt nothing bad could touch us. It seemed natural to be
with him in a dangerous place.

We walked slowly through the park, stopping at Strawberry Fields. Stephen expressed his love of the Beatles and
his sadness over the death of John Lennon, who had lived
nearby in the Dakota. Stopping at the pond, we looked up
at the stars. It was all hokey and romantic stuff, but it was
working on every one of my cells. We climbed, laughing,
on the Alice in Wonderland sculpture, and then Stephen
beckoned me into a dark area off the main road. No, it's
not what you think; he wanted to show me a sculpture of a
wolf that was his special favorite. There, he told me of the
love he felt for his childhood dog, Comet, and as he was
talking, something very strange began to happen to my
senses. Everything slowed down as it had in the bathroom
at the café. I became acutely aware of everything about
this man: the exact pitch of his voice, his quiet attention
when I spoke, and the sounds his boots made when he
walked on the outside edges of his feet. His strides were
long like mine, his intention deliberate. He was in no rush.
I had heard of people going weak in the knees when
falling in love; I found myself weak from head to toe, and
as alert as I had ever been in my life. When we finally held

hands, the blood left my arm. I was so enlivened by his touch it nearly frightened me.

It must have been 4 A.M. when we surfaced from the darkness of the park. We never encountered another soul. For that brief, enchanted time, Central Park was ours. At the steps of my five-story walk-up apartment, on Ninetieth Street, we kissed for the first time. My senses were so electrified that I can still feel the touch of his crisp blue shirt against my palms and the solid weight of him beneath it. I felt the starch of his shirt, the grain of the heavy cotton, and the hardness of his upper arm. Even in the economy of our touch, I felt a passion beyond any lovemaking I had experienced. I was overwhelmed, unable to take any more sensation. I asked him to please leave me and go home. He wondered if he had done something wrong, though everything about me must have been screaming out that he'd done just right. I stammered, "I like you way too much and you just have to go now." I turned and ran the five flights of stairs, leaving this man I didn't want to leave holding the stair rail. When I got to my rooms, I peeked out the window and found him looking up at me. I prayed he would understand me as I watched him walk away, hands in his pockets.

You won't be surprised to learn that we met again the next evening, and needless to say, I didn't send him home that night or any other after that. We married eight months later and have been together eighteen years since. That period of courtship was the bridge between daydreaming about a life in Paris and what has developed into the life I cherish and the family I love. I never knew that love could hurt, but for months we would look at each other knowing

With Stephen on our wedding day

the pain of intense, almost inexpressible love. We might wish for it to ease up so that we could breathe, but we were aware that the pleasure-pain of new love is a temporary gift worth feeling to the fullest as long as it lasts.

Yoga can be the thing that brings back those feelings of breathless love for me. I raise my spine, lifting it until it contracts and slightly constricts my breath. When I release, there is a rush of exhilaration that fills my body. It feels very pure to me, reminding me that love is universal, unconditional, belonging to us all. That is why a story like mine is as common as couples, yet unique and powerful to the people involved every time. We don't all find lasting love with a soul mate, and in all but the rarest cases love eventually evolves into life and routine and comfort. But if I refresh my spirit, there is really tremendous pleasure in the growth and transformation of my relationship. In my yoga and, even more important, in my meditation, I find endless, unfading joy that comes from God and spirit. It envelops me. I use the postures to calm my body and find peace so that I am open to the revelation of bliss.

9

SHOULDER STAND,

OR *SALAMBA SARVANGASANA*

Shoulder Stand is considered the mother of all the poses and it is a favorite of mine. It has the odd double effect of invigorating my whole body while also soothing, cooling, and nourishing. I like to do it near the end of a yoga session because the cooling effect helps lead me into my meditation. Many people find it necessary to place blankets under their shoulders for this pose, but blankets make me feel completely unstable. In case you haven't gotten the picture yet—give me that contact with the ground! Anyway, it is a personal choice.

I lie on my back, aligning and straightening, and then bend my knees so that my feet are placed hip-width apart near my buttocks. I press my shoulders into the earth, drawing my shoulder blades toward my waist. This action of pulling my shoulders underneath gives me a feeling that my upper back is lifting off the floor, though everything is still pressing downward. Turning my palms up, I extend my arms down by my sides, flat on the floor. My elbows are close in beside my waist, back ribs moved in. On an exhale, I press my elbows into the floor and swing my bent legs up over my head. My hands come up to support my lower back, thumbs clasping around my sides, fingers pointing down my sacrum. I check my position, making sure that my shoulders are still firmly underneath me because I always want to be on my shoulders and not my neck. This is a Shoulder Stand, not a neck stand! Sure that I am correctly supported, I lengthen my legs straight up to the sky and feel blood pouring down into my body. It cools and soothes me. I move my breastbone toward my chin, feeling a slight pressure on my throat and the thyroid, at the base of my neck. I concentrate on sending vitality to that poor, somewhat handicapped gland. It has been a victim of my many experiments with diet, and the story of those experiments, which I have alluded to here and there in this book, is as clear a window as I can give you into what it is like to live with an obsessive, compulsive mind like mine.

When my mother got cancer, I swallowed my twelve-year-old's needs and fears and became the parent searching for answers. I soon decided that food was the great key, the most critical influence on our health. Healthy eating had to be equivalent to healthy living, and for me it was natural to make the leap to thinking that the healthier my eating was, the healthier *I* would be. The only problem was that I had no idea what the body or the mind really needed for fuel. My main source of information in those days was John Robbins's *Diet for a New America: How Your*

Food Choices Affect Your Health, Happiness and the Future of Life on Earth. It is a brilliant book, full of exactly the kind of stuff I wanted to know. I was convinced that a strict vegetarian diet was right for me and right for the planet. Much to my Idaho-born, steak-and-potatoes mother's dismay, I ate no more meat, no fish, no chicken, no eggs. Basically, I ate a lot of cereal. Boxes of it. Soon, I became a vegan. If serious vegetarianism was good, extreme vegetarianism had to be better, right? So I ate frightening big bowls of cereal with apple juice on it instead of milk. For lunch, I had salad without dressing, which I considered horribly fatty. This would leave me still starving, so I scarfed down bowls of burnt popcorn. I guess burnt popcorn appealed to my senses because its flavor had a little more substance than the blandness of straight, unbuttered corn. Anyway, this was my diet for many, many years, and what distinguished my way of eating from your garden variety food faddist's was the dedication I brought to the job of starving my body. I loved bread. I'd been known to eat an entire loaf at one sitting, so I gave up wheat and bread completely. One by one, I hunted down all my cravings and tried to exterminate them. All but one.

I was clueless that no matter how much airy carbohydrate I put into my body, there was nothing to hold it there. The carbs immediately turned to sugar in my overaerobic body, giving me a brief rush of energy and then a major crash. That's when my addiction to caffeine began. I discovered coffee at seventeen while living alone in New York. Coffee filled the energy gaps between the carbohydrate/sugar crashing. Soon, I was grinding, brewing, and sipping espresso—hot, with vanilla, foamed, iced, and frothy. I began to think of coffee as my one indulgence, my one vice. And because it was my only vice, I had no ability to control it. To this day, I'd love to be able to enjoy a cup of coffee occasionally, a gelato in Italy, or a sip of champagne on my anniversary. I'd love to be able to honor the celebration of special events with a treat; but once I start, small treats don't satisfy me. If I can have one iced espresso, I can have them every day. In fact, why not three times a day? In no time, I am an addict looking for a fix.

I had moved to New York to get away from the pressures of being the only one living at home with my mother. Dad was mostly an absentee fisherman, and Muffet and Margaux were in and out, traveling the world. I fancied myself an adult and was able to impose that belief on my parents as well. I suppose that my case for being able to care for myself was plausible because I was never a problem for them. After all, I'd never called for a ride home past midnight, stoned and unruly. I rarely went out when I wasn't home by ten-thirty. There was hardly any boy interest on the horizon. I was a boring teenager because I was afraid not to be. Boring meant I was in control. Boring went hand in hand with policing what went in my mouth as a means of control. And having control meant I wouldn't get cancer like my mom or heart disease like Dad. If I never took drugs, I wouldn't go crazy like Muffet, and if I ate carefully and avoided both drugs and alcohol, I wouldn't get emotional problems or gain weight like Margaux. I had it wrapped up in a concise little package—order, discipline, and control in all issues would prevent problems with my body and mind.

Having very little spiritual training at that time, I

didn't realize that I couldn't really control things in my life through sheer will, though I gave it a good try. The depth of my will let me influence matters strongly, and that masked the real truth for a long time. Today, I believe that will can be a powerful tool for healthy habits, but it won't allow me to rewrite my destiny without a much deeper understanding of why I do the things I do. Slowly, I have been uncovering the fears that drive me, and in the process learning to love and forgive myself. It seems now that my early choice of will was a pure survival technique. It kept me sane and alive at a time when neither was a sure thing for somebody with my emotional and biological heritage.

Endless bowls of burnt popcorn were filling not only my stomach, but also my loneliness: the chewing and swallowing were soothing my feelings of abandonment. Somehow, when my parents agreed to let me move to Manhattan alone at sixteen, I felt they were giving me away too easily. They seemed not to care enough to parent me and insist that I stay home and finish high school as other kids had to do. Today, when my own girls ask to do inappropriate things, like driving the Los Angeles freeways with their sixteen-year-old cousin or moving to New York to study dance, I know that they are ultimately relieved to be told no, or given a timeline for when those actions will be all right. Giving children limits makes them feel loved. My parents did what they thought was best, but they had been terribly beaten up by my sisters and their constant testing of boundaries. When I began to test them in turn, they just seemed tired. I realize now that they loved me, but in those days I thought they didn't care. Parenting is exhausting and relentless, but as a parent I know that I have to be there when it matters because the effects are everlasting.

Alone in New York, I ate myself happy and, as I thought, healthy. I was following the extremely low-fat Pritikin diet. I was never bulimic like Margaux since I was too afraid of throwing up—the ultimate loss of control. I wasn't anorexic, either. I loved eating too much for that. So bingeing was the order of the day, followed by purging fasts and detoxifying herbal teas. The fasts were two- or three-day water-and-coffee affairs in my studio apartment. I would sit, hollow, empty, and buzzing, obsessing about the foods I would allow myself when I resumed eating. I had no idea that my starved metabolism was learning to go into slow motion, to store fat every time I ate. Since then, I have discovered that when I fast long and frequently, my body gets the message that I am starving. An annual spiritual or cleansing fast can be great, but when I fasted constantly my metabolism slowed down to conserve what little fuel my cells had. So, when I ate again my body didn't go back to normal speed; instead it stored the food as fat to prepare for the next famine. I was like a Neolithic hunter-gatherer, fattening up during the warm months to prepare for a long, cold freeze.

Years of this kind of feast-and-famine took a toll on me. I didn't get fat, because my caloric intake was so scanty, but I was losing muscle mass because of the lack of protein. The constant carbohydrate/sugar loading didn't meet my body's needs, so it began to eat at itself, digesting muscle and brain cells. My energy was terrible and my moods were all over the place. But my only thought was to solve the problem through more determination and self-denial. By my early twenties, I was heavily into the Fit for Life program. This added the element of rigorous food combining to my vegan diet. Now, I believe awareness of how we are affected by the combination of foods we eat is very beneficial, especially for people with an ailing digestive system. But for an obviously obsessive-compulsive person like me, food combining just became another fixation. I ate fruit all morning, sometimes all day, and nothing else, except caffeine, of course. In the evenings I had a huge salad with fat-free dressing and either popcorn or a baked potato. If it was one of my rare protein days, I would have tofu or fish. But always I ate fruit alone, or vegetables with either carbohydrates or protein. Carbohydrates and protein never went together—never.

My opinion was that my eating habits were extremely healthy. I thought, I eat only organic fruits and vegetables and a little bit of tofu or fish. I'm going to live forever. By dinner, though, my adrenals and nervous system were so blown out by sugar and stimulants that I was exhausted and famished. I didn't smoke or drink, so I'd have another espresso. I couldn't imagine giving it up. The hair-raisingly bad diet pattern seemed to be here to stay—until I got pregnant and my body's wisdom temporarily overruled my mind.

It is a real blessing that our bodies and spirits have a way of taking care of us when we have "a bun in the oven." My gravid body screamed about its needs and I listened, correctly for once. I couldn't look a cup of coffee in the face. My consumption of eggs, free-range chicken, and salmon was so huge that there were raised eyebrows among friends and family—except my mother, who loved the way I ate when I was pregnant with Dree. She couldn't stop praising me for "eating normal again." She was right. My baby needed the protein and fats, but I truly think that my own body was crying out for that sustenance, too. I had more energy while I was pregnant than I'd had since I was a girl. The energy was steady, as well, without the harrowing dips and unstable moodiness that had been my pattern. I felt great.

You would think that I'd learned my lesson, but I didn't put it together after the girls were born—maybe I didn't really want to. Denial is a great place to hang out if you have an addictive personality. I'm just glad that my addictions were relatively harmless; being overstuffed on lettuce and fruit or even hyper on caffeine wasn't going to kill me, though it wasn't doing me any favors. Twenty-two years of eating on the excessive side of the health pendulum had so messed up my metabolism that I developed thyroid disease. The gland basically shut down. No thyroid means no energy. The problem was diagnosed through blood tests at age thirty-seven, and I was put on a regimen of natural thyroid hormone. Within a few months, I started to feel better.

Dr. Peter Evans, the holistic doctor who had discovered the sad state of my thyroid, took advantage of having my full attention to suggest that I start eating some more protein along with my hormonal supplement. I was still coffee freebasing throughout the day, but I began having egg whites at breakfast, coffee for lunch, and high-protein dinners without fat or carbohydrates. For me it was an improvement, and my energy levels were markedly better.

I believe Dr. Evans would have insisted I give up coffee if he knew how badly I was abusing it. I routinely skipped meals in favor of iced, blended espressos with vanilla—no milk, no sweetener. I was healthy, remember? I even started mixing instant organic (of course!) coffee with ice in a blender, creating thick foam that I would eat with a spoon, in place of meals. The blender whipped so much air into the concoction that it filled me up and got me buzzed simultaneously. It seemed so healthy—no calories, organic coffee—I'm a saint! Sadly for my contribution to world cuisine, the coffee foam filled my upper intestine with so much air that I developed an embarrassing belching problem. My friends were kind enough not to mention how bizarre this new habit was. They had seen me through enough weirdness that they must have sighed and thought, This too shall pass. It did, but it wasn't my idea.

On October 15, 2000, after a peaceful meditation at the Self-Realization Fellowship Temple in Pasadena, Dr. Evans sat me down outside the Wild Oats health food store and broached the idea of a new eating program for me. Since he is my doctor and spiritual teacher, I am more inclined to listen to him on matters of health and lifestyle than to anybody else, but what he was saying sounded like a total overhaul. He told me that my unguided years of compulsive "healthy" eating had broken my body down, causing my thyroid problem and opening the door to degenerative diseases like those that had afflicted my parents. The warnings about what might happen if I kept on following the same diet were pretty dire. I was alarmed, but my body understood that he was telling the truth. All my lifelong attention to diet had been aimed at making myself healthier, so I plunged ahead and told Dr. Evans that I was game for whatever changes he would suggest. I had no idea what I was agreeing to do in the next half hour of grocery shopping!

As we entered the store, I was thinking that it would be nice to be more normal, to eat the things other people eat. It sounded as if Dr. Evans was proposing a diet like the one my mother followed when I was a child, minus the alcohol. He waltzed through the tidy aisles in sections of the market I'd rarely visited. He was gathering food into his cart that was new to me, with the strong implication that I should follow his example. It was typical of him. He never tells his patients what to do; he explains the pros and cons and lets us come to our own conclusions. Always the good girl, I picked up everything he did. It began fairly gently. Butter—*I buy that for the girls,* I thought to myself. Whole eggs—*wow, no more bottled egg whites!* Then heavy cream—my hand was shaking when I pulled that off the refrigerated shelf! He moved quickly on to hormone-free steak and I followed suit, clearing my drying throat as I ordered it from the butcher. "Why red meat?" I managed to croak. He replied that I needed it until my B_{12} and folic acid levels came up to normal. My body actually needed it! Then he moved into more familiar territory in the bread section, picking a flourless sprouted-grain loaf. Next came organic string cheese and loads of organic vegetables. *Phew! This I could handle.* Then he unsettled me again by mentioning the critical need to snack. "Snack?" I panicked. All I could think was, *I don't snack.*

Dr. Evans said, "I eat three meals a day and two snacks, and the only thing I monitor is my carbohydrate intake."

Suddenly, it was all starting to seem impossible. My mind was racing, looking for a way out. *Oh boy, I can't deal with this. Five times of grazing every day? I only know how to eat twice, and those meals are just my air foods. If I eat five times a day on this food I'm going to turn into a five-ten-and-a-half Amazon.*

Dr. Evans's voice broke through my chattering. "Do you want a bag of cashews, too?" he asked.

"Yeah. Sure." I almost choked on my reply as I took a bag of the hugely fattening little crescents that would almost surely kill me.

After we cleared the checkout line and were pushing our carts toward our cars, I found myself leaning into my cart as if it were a walker. Visions of fat and age were pushing me down to the oil-stained pavement. I felt my blood stopping. Dr. Evans came to my rescue by mercilessly appealing to my compulsive mind—he handed me a printout of my new diet program. It is based on the research of Drs. Ron Rosedale and Diana Schwarzbein, who have pioneered new dietary approaches to treating diabetes, obesity, and heart disease. They believe that the low-fat, high-carbohydrate diets commonly recommended for people with these diseases actually contribute to illness. The lack of healthy fats starves the cells, while the overdose of carbohydrates is rapidly turned to sugar in the body. The flood of sugar knocks insulin levels so far out of whack that the cells become resistant to that hormone, and any sugars not immediately needed for energy are stored as harmful fat deposits. To avoid this chain of problems, the dietary program recommends a balanced diet rich in healthy fats, with careful control of carbohydrate intake—the very opposite of the whole organizing idea I'd clung to for decades!

Dr. Evans's program had lists of foods containing

carbohydrates and their weights. I was to start with heavy restrictions—no more than fifteen grams at each meal and seven and a half grams per snack—at least until my body, fed more protein and fat, believed I wouldn't be starving it anymore. When my sugar, hormone, and stimulant levels were under control, I could think about increasing carbs again. As he turned to go he casually remarked, "Oh Mariel, one more thing. The coffee habit? That is the A-number-one thing that has got to go. Nothing else can even begin to get sorted out until you quit."

I left in a daze, thinking, Not only do I have to eat butter, eggs, cream, and snacks of nuts five times a day—I get no coffee. No buzz. No hollow, empty feeling. I may have no energy, and I'm edgy at times, but I'm skinny and in control.

My world seemed to be shaking apart at the seams. Every one of my old fears started to rage inside. Strange as it may seem, beginning this new program was one of the hardest things I ever had to do, and a battle raged inside myself. On the outside I always acted as if I was happy with my new diet, knowing that this was a far healthier food picture to paint for my growing girls. I didn't want them to end up with food and body issues like mine. Inside, though, I hated it. Most of the major crises in my life didn't cause nearly as much anxiety as eating balanced food did. I was an emotional wreck. The caffeine-withdrawal headache went on for two months. As my body began to have sufficient fuel to produce and regulate hormones, I started to have hot flashes—me, the girl who hadn't felt warm in years. I loathed the feeling of being full all the time. I missed being hungry, missed my buzz. I was horrified when

I looked in the mirror and saw hips reflecting back at me. My small breasts weren't so small anymore, and the healing process had created a thickness around my waist. My body was putting on weight because it was so sure I was going to starve it again soon that it was saving for a future cold, hungry day. It took over a year before my body trusted me enough to let go of the protective insurance.

So, I did the program and I did it like the compulsive champ I am. Two buttered eggs for breakfast with fruit or buttered toast; a snack of string cheese and half an apple; lunch of salad with *lots* of dressing and a piece of chicken or fish; afternoon snack in the fat country of cashews or peanut butter with celery; and a dinner quite similar to lunch. I came to love the taste of the food, but the weight drama was killing me. I would stand in front of my mirror and literally beg my image to let me go back to the way I was before. You have to realize that I wasn't just seeing ten pounds plastered around my middle; I was seeing Margaux in rehab or Muffet depressed and on the wrong medicine— fat was the ultimate loss of control. Fat also meant ugly in Hollywood, and it is a mean town when it comes to that. I was sure I'd never get a job again. It felt different and wrong. So, there in front of the mirror I could see my lifetime measure of control slipping away because of a decision I had to make over and over, every day.

Friends would compliment me about how lovely I looked and I would think, Sure, "lovely" is a word for big, fat, happy girls. I could neither get over my obsession about body image nor believe that anybody liked the way I looked. I meditated for hours to get relief from my head. When the time came to repeat my blood tests I wasn't sure whether

I wanted good results or bad, but the lab report showed that the first few months on the program had produced healthy results. My natural thyroid production was coming up, so the dosage of medication was lowered. My cholesterol level, which had been a scary 270 when I ate no fat, was dropping rapidly. And when I wasn't beating myself up, my energy was much better. Plus, I was getting a regular period for the first time in my life. I was healing physically even though I was still rebelling mentally.

I'm not sure how long I would have continued wrestling with all my old demons if life hadn't intervened, as it has a habit of doing. My father died and my husband got cancer and self-indulgent Mariel had to back up and get her priorities straight. I said to myself, This is an old issue. It's time to move on now. If I'm heavier, maybe it's because I'm meant to be. With all the drama around me, I was generally absorbed outside my personal worries. I used my will to slap myself back into shape whenever I would start getting insecure about my figure. Traumatic as they were, the distractions helped me with my personal problems. Relieved from the everyday agonizing, I made a quiet accommodation with my new diet and my new self. After I became confident about the principles behind the thing, I made adjustments that suit me. For instance, cheese and heavy cream simply don't agree with me, so I stopped eating them. I know that I don't *have* to eat nuts for a snack. I can boil an egg or take a few bites of turkey. The point is not to overeat five times a day; I just want to provide myself with consistent nutrition that acts like a drip system in my body. That way, I don't let my adrenaline, serotonin, or insulin levels get screwy.

As for coffee, once in a while I cheat and have some organic green tea, but only once in a while. I can hear you saying that green tea is a healthy source of beneficial antioxidants, but with my addictive personality I can take "healthy" and turn it into an out-of-control train wreck. I have to accept the fact that I am a certified caffeineaholic in recovery.

Since my acceptance of eating this way I have lost the extra ten pounds, yet kept a more feminine look that others seem to find attractive. I'm still unsure. Unquestionably, the biggest plus is a satisfying consistency of mood. I wouldn't trade this newfound sense of balance even for an iced blended espresso. The feeling of physical and mental peace is a gift. I suppose that is why I chose Shoulder Stand as the yoga pose to introduce this chapter about eating. It is a pose of nourishment and acceptance, and its soothing, cooling-down quality epitomizes the kind of delight I cherish these days in my practice and in my life.

10

DOG TILT AND CAT TILT

I have to admit that because of my short-circuited childhood, I am still looking to capture my full allotment of childlike joy and abandon. I finally am learning to play—entering middle age and learning to play! My daily yoga practice often begins with Dog Tilt and Cat Tilt, two lighthearted poses that really merge into one funny, joyful movement. I'm not even sure if serious yogis have dignified these poses by conferring Sanskrit names on them. Whatever they are really called, though, in the early morning they loosen the joints and muscles of my back like a great stretch. They feel good.

I start on all fours on my mat, with my back forming a tabletop. My hands are outstretched in front and my toes are pointing to the back. On an inhale I reach my head, neck, and upper back toward the sky while simultaneously lifting my butt back and up. When I take that inhale, I use the whole breath to reach the full extension of the stretch; at the same time my middle and lower back are compressing into an arch. The front side of my body awakens. When I exhale, the action is reversed. My head and neck are lowered and my back arches up like a Halloween cat yowling at the full moon. I don't want to feel like a scared cat; instead I picture a luxuriating feline stretching out the entire length of her spine in a warm patch of sunshine. I'm trying to hollow my belly, feeding breath and energy into my slowly awakening spine. These postures were part of the reduced yoga workouts I did while I was pregnant with our girls, though my hollowed belly was then more a fantasy as I shifted my precious passenger first forward and then back. Sometimes along with arching up and down, I go sideways like a dog wagging its tail. When I'm feeling particularly frisky, I may have music on, wagging side to side, up and down, and around in circles. If I can forget to be embarrassed, forget to be a grown-up, the unstructured movement gives me a childlike feeling of delight.

After I married Stephen, in 1984, my film career sort of went on simmer. There was work, but my energies were turned to our marriage and our new life together in New York. I made *The Mean Season* with Kurt Russell while still courting Stephen, and soon after our marriage played the role of protégée to Peter O'Toole's eccentric scientist in *Creator*. The most enjoyable film of this period, though the movie itself was terrible, was *Superman IV: The Quest for Peace*. I loved working with Gene Hackman, who played the evil genius Lex Luthor, and Christopher Reeve, Superman himself, is the quintessential gentleman. In fact, the whole cast was great and the experience of living in London was wonderful. It just goes to show that the experiences of the people making a movie can be totally different from what the audience feels in the theater viewing the finished film. I'm afraid some critic said it would have been better if the budget for the whole film had been donated to charity!

When Stephen and I returned to New York, he expressed dissatisfaction with his business. He was pouring his time and energy into the Hard Rock Café and not getting much in return. I encouraged him to start his own place, so we soon found ourselves setting up a restaurant called Sam's Café on Eightieth Street and Third Avenue. Surprisingly, Sam's was named after me. Handling celebrity is a bit of a trick, and Stephen hated it when people stared at us anytime he called my name in public. He had taken to calling me Sam in self-defense.

We were a good team in the restaurant business. Stephen built the business and I designed an interior of simple Americana: cow signs and quilts on the walls; clean, good food on the tables. We thought of it as "food you'd want at home but didn't have the time to make." The menu featured things like grilled fish and meat, meat loaf, fried chicken, mashed potatoes, and amazing salads: some comfort food mixed with grazing fare for the likes of me. Stephen had to sweat over the business on a daily basis, while I had the fun job of coming in and enjoying the place we had made. It became quite the hot spot on the Upper East Side, a development that eventually led to the opening of Sam's Restaurant in the Equitable Life Insurance Building, on Fifty-second Street between Sixth and Seventh Avenues. The midtown place was huge and also successful, but running restaurants is a tiring business. It was as if Stephen were in a play that never closed, night after night, with no middle and no end. He worked while I slept. At one point, we had a Sam's in Dallas, Houston, Miami, and Los Angeles, and poor Stephen was sprinting around the country. But I'm getting ahead of my story.

One day in early 1987, while we were still just working in New York, I got a call from Blake Edwards in Los Angeles. He was making a film called *Sunset* with the hot new television star Bruce Willis and veteran James Garner. He said he wanted me to audition for a part. After a tryout, Blake cast me in the part of Cheryl King and immediately told me to cut off my hair and dye the buzz dark brown. I was devastated. Past experience taught me that my face looked awful with short hair. I begged to be allowed to wear a wig like practically every other member of the cast, but Blake was adamant. He wanted my blond locks shorn. So, I dutifully went to the hairdresser and emerged hating the way I looked. It upset me so deeply that I began to feel nauseous all the time. In fact, I seemed to be overreacting completely. I mean, it was a haircut! And I was sick to my stomach every day! Finally it dawned on me that something else might be going on. I went to the doctor and it was confirmed that I was pregnant. I had always wanted children, so I was over the moon with excitement. Yet with all the joy and anticipation, I spent the first twelve weeks of my pregnancy on a film set feeling like I was going to lose my cookies any minute.

I managed to keep myself together with an easy hatha yoga practice and lots of breathing. Only while doing yoga or eating did I feel all right. My routines were simple: Sun Salutation; Mountain and a version of it with the feet and

Sunset, *and that dark hair*

arms spread, called Tree; Warrior; and a number of sitting postures. Pregnant-lady yoga is something best done with guidance from an experienced adviser, and my vocabulary of postures wasn't very large at the time, but I'm sure it was beneficial to maintain the length and suppleness of my limbs. It just seemed natural to me to breathe into my joints and hips while my body opened and softened for the impending birth, and the breath work was perfect preparation for Lamaze training.

Near the end of filming *Sunset,* Stephen and I decided that we would move back to Idaho for the birth of our child. We loved the idea of the clean, healthy environment and the prospect of a quiet, friendly hospital. The log cabin was too remote and without electricity or phone. So, when the shoot was finished, we drove straight to Sun Valley to look for a house. Everything was frighteningly expensive. Sun Valley has always been a fashionable place, of course, and I just *had* to live north of town, where I'd grown up. On that side, the homes are backed up against stunningly beautiful national forest land at the foot of the Sawtooth Mountains, with prices to match the scenery.

Miraculously, we quickly found our dream house—way out of our price range. It was owned by Barbara Minty, who is Steve McQueen's widow. During his tenure there he had blasted bullet holes in the ceiling of the dining room. It was all terribly intriguing for Stephen, who is a huge McQueen fan; he loved that manly image. Ironically, the modest log house seemed sweet to me, and the five acres along the Big Wood River seemed even sweeter. Without too much hope, we made an offer that we could afford but that was way below the asking price. To our amazement Barbara accepted. We were stunned. From the moment I heard, I knew we were meant to own this place. It felt so right.

I immediately set about building a nest, part of which involved finding a baby doctor I liked and taking all the recommended blood tests. Here, a dark cloud appeared on the horizon. The doctor called me in to tell me that my maternal serum alpha fetoprotein levels were low. Fetoprotein is produced by the fetus and small amounts of it cross the placenta into the mother's bloodstream. Abnormal levels can mean trouble: too much can indicate neural tube defects or spina bifida; too little, such as I had, may mean Down syndrome. The doctors wanted me to have an amniocentesis, a procedure usually reserved for women older than my twenty-six years. It certainly made me feel vulnerable. A long, hollow needle was inserted into my uterus and the amniotic sac surrounding my dear baby. Fluid was withdrawn so it could be analyzed for chromosomal defects, a procedure that, in those days, took four agonizing weeks of waiting before the results came back.

We decided to distract ourselves by attending the premiere of *Superman IV* in London. The festivities were nice, but we couldn't escape our worries. On a park bench in a quaint little square near our London hotel we sat together and talked about whether we were ready to provide the nurturing for a child who might not be normal. Sobbing together, we decided that we would have our baby, no matter what. If we were meant to care for a child with Down syndrome, then we figured we could help him or her more than most, and we were grateful. Making the decision seemed to help us get on with life. I donned my strapless black evening gown, designed to hide my swelling tummy, and smiled as we were introduced to Prince Charles and Princess Diana. It was exciting and elegant to curtsy for the royals. I sat beside the prince as we watched the silly film, and he kept it all in perspective by talking quietly to me during the screening about nature and architecture. No need to keep silent during *that* film!

After it was all over, Stephen and I flew home together, realizing on being alone again that we were both holding our breath in anticipation of the test results that awaited us. We were lucky. The news was wonderful! Everything seemed normal, and my uncle, who had a blood lab in Boise, even threw in the information that the baby was a girl. At last we could focus on the fun of what was coming. I began a routine of hiking Mount Baldy, practicing yoga, and meditating. Meditation was fairly new for me, but I believed the calmness I felt could only be good for my baby. After exactly four months I stopped having the morning—no, all-day sickness—I had been suffering. All of a sudden I was full of energy. My system was revving with masses of extra blood. I was eating well for a change, with protein, organic vegetables and grains, and no caffeine. I felt like a dynamo. There was no mountain I couldn't climb. Early in the pregnancy I gained about eight pounds and then my weight stabilized with very little further change despite the relatively huge meals I was eating. The flow of my simple yoga was full of smiles inside my skin. My moods were level and easy. I loved being pregnant!

The only strange craving I developed was for mustard, which I put on absolutely everything. To this day there is not a meal where I don't have mustard on the side. It is a joke among my friends. I'd like to think it comes from some strange biblical association, but I can't imagine what that would be. Knowing my history of having to give up vices, I am fully prepared for the day when some wise adviser tells me that my little obsession with mustard has to go, but until then—French's, I'm yours!

The loveliest part of being pregnant was the amazing awareness I had of everything about my body. Hiking in the mountains, I could specifically feel the different muscles in my legs contracting at the same time that I felt the weight of my new addition settling down onto my hips. Rather than uncomfortable, the pressure on my sacrum made me feel stable in my back. Sometimes while walking the trails I could feel shifts in my belly as my baby girl found comfort in another position. She was always moving with the hours of hiking. I hoped she could breathe in the beauty of the day with me—summer air filled with the scents of pine, grass, and heat. I knew it would be years before she could hike along with me on her own two feet, and I thought, This is my gift to her now. So, we walked our way through summer and into the cool, darkening fall. In the mornings we practiced asanas on the deck outside.

I grew even closer to my elbowing little girl through meditation with music. I had no formal instruction in the art of meditation, but found quiet Windham Hill pieces to be a perfect aid to sitting in contemplation. I simply focused on filling both mom and babe with love and peace. We had named her Dree while we were still courting. The sound of her name fills Stephen's earliest memory of this life, so he had always dreamed of his Dree. I hoped that she would lead a life filled with confidence and the esteem of others. I also hoped I wouldn't replay any of the tapes from my childhood for her.

As my due date approached, the doctors became worried that I had gained only fifteen pounds. My mother had never gained much with any of us, but that didn't comfort my physicians. The baby might not be getting enough nutrition! I was told that my labor had to be induced three weeks early—the sooner the better. In my body I felt that everything was fine, but I was happy at the thought of having my treasure in my arms, talking to her sweet face instead of to my belly. So I agreed and took a dose of labor-inducing hormones early on the morning of December 4, 1987. Stephen was in New York taking care of our restaurants. He dropped everything and ran for the airport, calling me nervously on the plane phone and again from Salt Lake City while he waited for the connection to Sun Valley.

One hitch in this new plan was that I'd had only one Lamaze class to prepare me for the ordeal of labor. I was confident that my yoga breathing and meditation would pull me through, and indeed, the first several hours of labor pains were easy. Then, suddenly, the pain kicked into a higher gear. On arriving at the hospital, I'd told my nurse that I was having my child naturally and that no drug should even come near me. Friends had joked throughout the pregnancy that I was such a nature girl, I would probably go out into a field like a pioneer wife and deliver the baby myself. I laughingly thought they were probably right. Well, I was about to discover what every mother who has had a child naturally knows—the pain is staggering. In no time, I went from the confident natural woman, practicing my breathing, to a madwoman looking for the culprit who was trying to kill me. That's probably why earlier generations kept the husband away during labor—to save the guilty party from the woman's wrath. It occurred to me that maybe I wasn't really having a baby, but being tortured to death. I still recall all the agony of both my labors. Who says you forget?

After seven hours of electric pain, I was still dilated only the same two centimeters I'd started with. I looked at the nurse during the brief respite between contractions and said, "I need something really bad. I can't handle this." She responded, with a smile that made me want to rip her face off, "Oh no. You don't want anything. You told me no matter what you say, you don't want any drugs." Another contraction hit and I couldn't reply. All I heard was my husband saying, "She doesn't want anything, but I sure do." Either he was a nervous new father or it was too many drugs in the sixties. Well, if nobody is going to help me, I thought, I'd better get busy and get this baby out or I may not survive. God bless the women who endure labor for thirty hours or more—you are made of tougher stuff than I am.

I began to focus all my energy on the meager opening I'd created for my baby's entrance. My thoughts became laserlike, all trained on the one idea of opening, opening, opening. The focus helped me remove myself from the pain. With my pointed attention, I went from two centimeters to ten in about ten minutes. The labor pains became pushing pains. Stephen, always the discreet gentleman, said, "Wow, darlin', it's like the barn doors just opened up." He had a video camera and, thank God, he didn't capture any of it. In his nervous-new-father state he shot a lot more footage of the ceiling and floor than of the actual birth. It's amazing he has turned out to be an accomplished documentary filmmaker.

So, as happens with hundreds of thousands of others every day on this planet, I gave birth, to my little Dree. She was extraordinary to me. She was small, just five pounds of pure beauty. I wouldn't let them take the incubator out of my room, and my request was honored, one of the advantages of being in a small town where there was only one other patient on that floor of the hospital. The night was gloriously sleepless. I stared at the wonder of her, snuggling as much as I dared, and crying with the joy of it all. Out the window I could see an enormous full moon, and inside, in the soft light, the delicate fingers of this amazing new person.

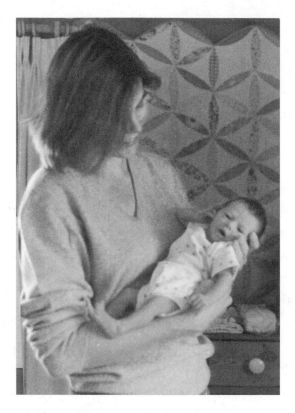

Becoming a mother; Dree at three days old

Dree was soon to become a delight for my mother. We had returned to New York and the business of the restaurants after her birth, but summer found us making the pilgrimage back to Sun Valley for a vacation in the mountains. Mom was light and easy around her granddaughter. She even complimented my performance as a mother, expressing joy over seeing me caring for a baby. Her demeanor was so different that I felt there had to be something even more behind it. She had spent so many years being angry and sick, and now it seemed that she was tired of fighting her life.

She had been very distant from me since I had fallen in love with Stephen. She seemed to feel that I'd abandoned her for the comfort and safety of a serious love even though I still spent great chunks of time with her. As difficult as she could be, I loved her, and in her bitter way, she adored me. I was her baby. So this loving summer was a period of mostly unspoken healing. Physically, she was very ill with a series of lung infections, but she didn't seem to have the same attitude toward her problems. She was accepting, even to the point of being kind to my father. After all these years, she was finally beginning to release from her fear and resentment; she was surrendering to God's plan for her.

One day Dree and I spent the afternoon and evening at her bedside. Dree was cooing and laughing at her playful grandmother. Mom made a particular point to tell me how much she loved me and that she knew I would always be a good mother. This kind of demonstrative, unsolicited kindness was so unusual that it struck me deeply, bringing tears to my eyes. I hugged her brittle, skinny body and cried some more. Her long fingers pushed aside hair from my face as only a mother can do, and she smiled such a loving smile. That was all—just a deeply loving smile. I watched her hands as she cuddled Dree, who found her pink fingernails irresistible. Those hands—those "capable hands," as she called them—were full of love. She said I had them too, and I did. I was happy to have her hands. They were hands that did things, that cleaned and scrubbed and cooked and comforted. If only her hands could have guided her life story it would have been a happier one. Dree and I left in a warm haze of love.

I was jarred awake by the telephone at 4:20 A.M. the following morning. Before Stephen could grab the phone, I knew that Mom was gone. We were just minutes away, so I was there by my father's side before the official world barged in on us. Muffet was there, too, looking at our mother's gnarled body lying on the bedroom floor, where she had fallen during a sudden bout of hemorrhaging that in moments had carried her off. I helped Dad move her back onto the bed, and looked closely at him to see how he was doing. He was businesslike. He had awaited this moment so long in his private nightmares that he wasn't registering much emotion. I knew a feeling of relief was building in him and I couldn't fault him for it. Their life together was rarely easy, but he was loyal, and as good to her as he could be.

We all had done our best to please her. I have to say it was Dree who pleased her most; or perhaps seeing me with Dree was what pleased her. In her first months on the planet this baby girl rekindled my mother's kind spirit. And their bond seemed to have an indefinable continuity after Mom died, because for several days, Dree awakened at exactly four-twenty and cried out as though she missed her grandmother. For my part, I was numb to the grief of my mother's death. I had cried so many tears, beginning with my childhood pleadings with God on her behalf, that I found myself barren of emotion when faced with her actual death. My grief remained dried up inside of me for years—until my father's death somehow released a flood of feelings for all my lost family.

A little more than a year after Dree's birth, I was pregnant again. The second go-around was very much like the first, except without all the worry. I had all-day sickness

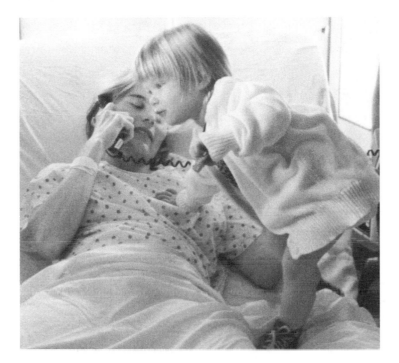

With Dree in the hospital right after Langley's birth

again, but knew that it would soon end. My blood feto-protein levels were low again but I took it in stride. I gained very little weight, but instead of fretting about it, took advantage by satisfying my huge urge to walk out in the mountains. The exposure to nature, to the sights and smells and weather, was like music to me and my growing baby. I walked every day, including my August due date, when I hiked nine miles. At the end, I was jumping up and down trying to start my labor.

On August 22, 1989, Langley Fox was born. The labor was far easier as I had prepared myself with proper Lamaze lessons and even had a labor coach—massage therapist who kept me focused. Stephen paced the room and joked while other close friends filmed the birth, turning the event into a documented joy. Dree was twenty-two months old and very much a part of bringing her baby sister into the world. Though she wasn't in the room at the moment of birth, she was stroking her sister in fascination only minutes afterward. They are bonded strongly to this day, though I notice that they have learned how to squabble over the years!

When the great event was over and I was left alone with this new treasure, I snuggled her close to my beating heart, listening to the tiny sound of her breathing. I remember the encompassing feeling of love and safety I felt as a child when my mother held me on her lap with my head to her breast. I heard her heart and felt the rise and fall of her breathing. It has always represented the epitome of mothering and pure love for me.

Every day, with my two girls, I ask to be given the necessary love and guidance for them. I am adamant that they see me as real, a person who makes ever so many mistakes but is willing to swallow her need to be right and apologize when her choices are poor. Parenting has become an illuminating mirror for observing myself. The girls bounce me back at myself in a clear, insightful, and sometimes difficult light. I have watched the rage of my mother come out—unseemly jealousy over seeing my girls filled with the very confidence and *joie de vivre* I prayed they would have. The little girl in me, who had to grow up too fast, never got to be like them. It hurts until I connect with the joy of realizing that I am no longer that sad little girl. I can watch my girls be expressive and free and well taken care of and know that is exactly how it ought to be. Nothing is a greater delight than a kind and happy child.

I may not have had the same kind of nurturing, but I had what I needed. I believe I needed a tougher childhood to equip me for the task of breaking out of the grip of my genetic makeup. It seems to me that we are likely to repeat the mistakes of our parents unless something happens to give us a major push into wanting a different understanding of life. In many ways, I was lucky to have landed in this life with a powerful desire for something more healthy and harmonious than I experienced at home. We can create new lives, new patterns, that can be passed on to our offspring. For me, it takes daily silence and constant awareness, but I don't want to get too heavy about it. That's where my kids help me. Sometimes I get to join in the giddy freedom of their youth. If I can open to it, there is great healing in reconnecting with my playful, easygoing side.

That's why Dog Tilt and Cat Tilt are perfect day breakers for me. Wriggling, writhing, and laughing aren't always the nature of my role as an adult. It's good to remind myself to play, and as my girls grow and make for themselves increasingly complex lives outside our family, I realize that I had better learn to play in my own life. I start that on my yoga mat. So today I'm a big kid moving through my postures, doing handstands and back bends with the curiosity and joy of a child.

11

SUN SALUTATION,
OR *SURYA NAMASKAR*

The Sun Salutation is a fluid series of movements linking together several of the basic postures I've been describing. When it goes well, it energizes me and brings heat into my body so that I can open up more easily in challenging poses. That's how it is supposed to be ... and yet each day is unique, and today is the day after the horrifying terrorist attacks on the World Trade Center and the Pentagon. Yesterday, doomed passengers struggled with the hijackers to crash a fourth plane in the Pennsylvania woods rather than hit some climactic target in Washington. I feel the grief and shock through all my body as I stand here in Mountain pose. It would be easy to return to the television or the telephone, but I have learned that the mere mechanics of my practice can be a gateway to calming my mind, to helping me find a path that leads me back to greater sanity. So I stand firm and raise my arms over my head, looking up at my hands and perhaps something beyond. It is a start.

The stretch of my arms feels good. I separate my hands, and while maintaining my strong legs and pulling my belly in, I fold down like a swan dive into a forward bend. There is no swooping gracefully to the floor today, though; the tight pain in my hamstrings makes me bend my knees. I'm cold, holding back from my feelings. The muscles are chattering, so I pause, just breathing. Normally my hands would be on the floor, but today they are straining to reach my shins. That's OK. I raise my head and lengthen my spine, inhaling deeply with the stretch. I hold it—then release down into the forward bend again. Here, in this first Salutation, is a flood of information about the state of my body, as if I needed it! The tenseness and distraction are trying to pull me out of myself, so I concentrate on my firmly planted feet as I pull my body up from the waist. Once again, I bring my hands to meet overhead, gazing gently and forgivingly on them before returning them to my sides in Mountain pose again. That completes a Half Sun Salutation.

The shortened Salutation makes sense to me this morning when my tightness is voicing its opinion. It is nice to be listening to my body and to feel in control of at least this one thing. I do three more Half Salutations, finding that each one reduces the screaming of my muscles. My breath is coming in as my arms move up, and going out as I bring my body down. I breathe in as I lengthen my spine, out as I go back into a fold, and in again as I lift my torso and arms to the sky. Subtle yet specific waves of energy are awakening in my body. It's almost as though I can feel my stagnant blood beginning to course and flow, like sand slowly pouring through the waist of an hourglass. The tightness is beginning to ease.

Getting comfortable in my body again, I decide to take the movement into a full Sun Salutation. Down I dive, hands fully to the ground now. I rise and lengthen, and as I begin coming forward into my second folding bend I take my right leg back into a deep lunge. My left leg is bent, and at a forty-five-degree angle to the floor, before I bring it back to meet the right in a perfect push-up position. Suddenly the energy has risen, and I stop to remind myself not to let my bum drop or rise too high. I pull my stomach in to create a strong center. This morning, gravity and grief are pulling my belly down, but I resist. Even on good days, creating this centeredness can be the most challenging part of my yoga practice. Today it is an outright struggle.

I ask myself if I can actually do a push-up and follow that into *Chaturanga Dandasana*, holding my entire body just above the floor with my elbows glued to my sides. Not yet on this morning. I will do the push up and then lower my legs to the ground. Touching the earth feels good. Slowly, I arch my upper torso into an easy back bend, toes extended. Then, curling my toes under, I raise myself into Downward Facing Dog. Mentally, the pull comes from my belly. My feet are adjusted hip-width apart and my hands are likewise planted as though in Mountain pose: solid, grounded, and splayed out. Breathing deeply and consciously, I feel connected to energy and my heart begins to beat faster.

Uninvited, the thought comes into my head that I'd like to be done soon today. I think my practice is going to be too hard. I didn't sleep well, I'm tired already, and I haven't even completed one full Salutation. My feeling of connectedness disappears and I'm anxious and upset by the thought of going on. *Whoa! Hold on here.* I tell myself to breathe more intently, to watch my panic at the impatience I'm feeling. I remind myself that it is OK to just keep breathing. Calming down a bit, I make the choice to do at least one more Salutation before I throw in the towel.

Sometimes, it blows me away that I can feel strong, centered, and excited one minute, and then, seemingly out of the blue, I'm nervous, impatient, and wishing I could run away the next. I guess much darker feelings literally flew out of the blue skies over the East Coast yesterday. And like far, far too many others, I have learned that these apparently random emotions can have deep roots in reality.

I am thinking back to June of 1995, when I was living full-time in Idaho with my family. The girls, Dree and Langley, were at the beginning of their summer vacation. We were planning a family adventure into the mountains, or perhaps a float trip on the Salmon River. Everything seemed rich and full of possibility, the summer stretching out far in front of us. But as we made our plans on June 29, I was completely out of sorts and emotional for no reason. No premenstrual excuses—nothing.

The girls wanted to cross the highway out front to go to a little convenience store for candy and lemonade: anything with sugar, since I don't keep much of it in the house. Stephen and I told them to take the dogs with them—Jazz, a big yellow Lab–shepherd mix, and Faboo, a little Maltese, who thought he was huge. They usually accompanied the girls everywhere, but this time the girls surprised us by saying they wanted to go without them. We insisted, so, against their instincts, the girls set off up the drive with the dogs running circles around them.

A minute later, struck by some terrible unease, Stephen and I looked at each other and wordlessly ran from the house toward the road. In the distance we saw the girls cross safely with Jazz in tow and Faboo lagging a little behind. And then, with a mounting sense of horror, we watched a speeding white pickup truck swerve to the side of the empty road to hit Faboo. I screamed in horror, looking at my hysterical girls, while Stephen desperately tried to read the culprit's license plate number. We were devastated, trying to revive our little dog through our tears. Stephen drove off at breakneck speed to the veterinarian, seven miles away, but it was a sad, futile trip with a dead dog. On the way home, piling disaster on disaster, a hawk flew smack into the windshield, falling dazed to the side of the road. Stephen stopped, miserable, and found that the bird was still alive. I have sometimes had success using homeopathic Rescue Remedy to revive songbirds that hit the windows of the house, so he gathered up the beautiful hawk and brought her home to me.

I began a long vigil, nursing the bird while the family prepared a teary burial ceremony for Faboo. All of my emotions from the day were focused on preventing any more death; they rose and fell as the bird seemed to respond and then faltered. My anguish was irrationally huge when the hawk died late in the day. I could hardly bear it. The next two days were the same. On the third day, we learned that my sister Margaux had died of an epileptic seizure on the same afternoon that I was nursing the hawk. Her body had just been found. I have always believed that a large part of

Muffet and Margaux in Sun Valley (after Margaux came out of rehab)

my grief looking into the bird's fierce eyes arose from a source I couldn't know.

The awful tragedy of Margaux's death came out of nowhere. She was as healthy as she had been in years, and her life was looking up. Our relationship had regained a trust and openness that we had lost. It was better than ever. We had visited together in Idaho a few months before, sharing some very sweet insights. We laughed and cried over the way we had played the complementary roles of rebel and good girl in order to survive in our strange family. We shared our mutual love of meditation and vowed to be close throughout our old age. I thank God we had those healing talks before I lost her.

I plunged into a state of emotional confusion after her death. Margaux was central to my definition of myself. She was not the person I wanted to be, because of the life she had chosen—or was given—to live, but we shared too many things for me not to identify with her. I was a little girl, looking carefully through big eyes, when she began being wild and also having her success. That may be why detachment and observation in my practice, and often in my life, come naturally to me.

At first, the family was told that Margaux died from an epileptic seizure brought on by an improper dosage of her medication. The doctors said this was compounded by her use of herbs that counteracted the epilepsy drugs. Then, a month later, the coroner released a sensational report finding that her death was a suicide. This prompted national headlines about "The Curse of the Hemingway Family." I was wounded and angry. The last thing I needed was to be told that I am part of an incurably sick and damned family. I wanted to show people my own healthy life, my family, and my obsession with exercise, meditation, and nourishing food. But Margaux's friends blamed me for not supporting her enough, and my father disappeared so far inside his grief that he became nearly invisible. Not only had he lost his baby; he was taken back to memories of himself as a young man whose father had just killed himself with a shotgun. We eventually completed our isolation by making a typically unhealthy family pact not to speak publicly about Margaux's life or death or any of it. Each alone, we went about our lives trying to be OK. It's what we always did, which may explain some of our problems.

I wasn't in denial so much as I was trying to figure out

who I am. Instead of feeling more like Mariel, able to distinguish myself from my sister, I became more confused about my own identity. I had always struggled to be myself, not Margaux—I wanted not to be as big as she was; I wanted to be known as the actress, not the model; I wanted to be the healthy one, not the alcoholic and drug addict. My mother always held her up as the example of what I should avoid in life. But when she died, instead of feeling that she was gone, I felt I really was her. I believed her problems were mine and my life was merely a cover-up, like a great costume. I feared I would have to become the sick person who lived inside me, carrying on the family curse. It was in my genes and in my destiny. Standing in the produce section of the local grocery store, I felt that I was about to melt to the floor beside the onions and lettuce and just cry, or scream out in fear and desperation.

Somehow, I didn't go crazy, even with all my biggest fears dancing in my head. I tried to use my meditation like a blanket from the cold, lost in my belief in God. Even there, in the serene quiet, I was pursued by my demons because Margaux had had incidents of psychosis years before, during long meditations in India. I knew that meditation was not at all the cause of her problems, but recalling the fact that she had attended a weekend-long workshop to become a kind of spiritual healer made me feel that I needed to protest, to assert that my spiritual life is legitimate and real and that I claim no special healing powers.

It was at this time that I realized the value of simply continuing my practice. While my sessions were definitely not inspired, they were organized and precise. I had difficulty with full, rich breath, and my sense of observation was not in tune, but I kept practicing and meditating. The mechanical asana work still calmed my body, allowing me to sit in meditation. Since the thoughts trying to overwhelm me were so powerful, I made my physical yoga practice very vigorous. The harder I worked physically, the easier my meditation became. I gradually began to let go of my fear of Margaux's karma, realizing that her pain and problems were hers and not mine. My spiritual teacher, Dr. Peter Evans, looked at me one day and said, "Mariel, you are not your sister... you are not your sister." He somehow understood how deeply I needed to hear those words from a trusted friend, and those simple words released me. Slowly, I reoccupied my own body in Ketchum, with two young daughters and a husband. I could breathe again.

Oddly, all through my exercise and hiking I seemed to be cold. I could never seem to do enough to warm my body. Afraid to feel, I was cold to my emotions and my practice reflected that. Only time and patience and a reopening heart cured me. The thing to remember is that we learn the most in times of difficulty. Knowledge accumulates clandestinely, revealing itself when the pain lifts. And so, I stand in Mountain pose, lifting my hands overhead, choosing to execute another Sun Salutation.

12

MEDITATION

Sitting in meditation is the yoga I live for. I may not always have time for a physical workout, but I meditate every day, needing it like oxygen. I sit in Lotus position with a blanket or cushion under me to elevate the base of my spine. The lift helps me keep my entire back straight, something I find necessary for successfully going deep. My hands are placed in the creases where my hips and legs meet, palms up, the tips of my index fingers and my thumbs resting gently together. My eyes are closed, but I'm gazing up and in toward the third-eye center between my brows—a place some call the point of Christ consciousness.

If I have done a hatha yoga practice, I find that I slip easily into a peaceful state. If not, then I often struggle to escape from the grip of my thoughts—those all-important thoughts that simply must be addressed right now. Or do they? I remind myself that if what I am concerned about right now is so bloody important, then I will likely remember it when I'm done sitting. I calm my brain, allowing the thoughts to come and allowing them to go without grabbing on to them. It takes all my concentration to surrender. I am so programmed to act on what is in my mind that I need help to escape the desire to do something, so I focus attention on my breathing. I make consciously deeper breaths at first, breaths so deep I can latch on to them. Gradually this removes my attention from the need to call the school counselor or to write down the crucial fact that I have to buy mayonnaise for the girls' sandwiches. Sooner or later, there is just breath going deeply in and completely out; my brain needs nothing more than the filling and relaxing of my lungs. The more I am alone with my breathing, the more I sink deeply inside myself. Over the years I have learned many breathing techniques, and I use whichever ones feel right on a given day; all of them are aids to help me quiet myself internally, body and mind. I want to reach an inner stillness that leads me to peace, because when I am truly peaceful I sometimes am able to reach beyond to connect with a sense of unconditional love—God's eternal joy.

It is impossible to write about things that cannot be spoken about—things that lie in realms where words have no use. But I want to try to express what it was about my life that made me so receptive to the peace and joy I experience when my meditation goes well.

I grew up thinking that it's absurd to say that we live difficult lives. That seems like a given to me. There are many pleasures in the world, yet every time I grasp one I soon find it to be empty, especially since I want to indulge excessively in anything good. My obsessive behavior is cut from the same cloth as all the other addictive substance-abuse tendencies in my family. We Hemingways are trying to find an easy way out of the pain and disappointment life serves up. I find that I am like the child who desperately yearns for a new toy—the new Malibu Barbie. I can scarcely imagine how happy I will be if only I can get it. But when I do get my blond, high-breasted doll, complete with her beach bungalow, it takes just a few minutes before Barbie's perfect body, cute home, and adoring partner, Ken, leave me cold. She's tossed in the corner with my last great *need-to-have-it* toy, soon to be replaced by the desire for something else.

It seems to me that before I discovered meditation I traveled from one want to the next, seeking comfort and joy in winning acting roles and the love of my peers, or even things as trivial as a silk carpet or the perfect physique. If I ran two miles and felt fabulous afterward, I would run two miles every day looking for the same high. When that failed, I would compulsively add miles, always hoping to get back to the original delight, until I exceeded my limits and hurt myself. Moderation is a lesson I must learn over and over again. Vegetarianism had a joyous, high effect on me when I started eating that way. When the original energizing effect waned, I stupidly added excess sugar and caffeine, turning coffee from a treat into an overdose. Even so, it never gave me the kick I'd enjoyed in the beginning. Love, too, has to survive the original intoxication's metamorphosis into mortgage payments, fighting kids, and the romantic experience of having your sweetie use the toilet while you're brushing your teeth. I have always wondered why we are put here dreaming of so much more than we are likely to find in daily life. For myself, I'm sure I was looking in all the wrong places.

Life gives us hints that our yearnings aren't completely crazy. All along, there have been rare moments when I directly felt the unconditional love that I now associate with my devotion to God. I remember climbing a peak in the Sawtooth Range, in the macho way I did it as a teenager, and being utterly stopped at the summit by the beauty of nature all around me. My skin still prickles with the memory of that cold October morning, and I can see the jagged mountains cutting into the overwhelmingly blue sky. But this moment is set off from all the other times the mountains have delighted me by the specific feeling I had of a loving intelligence in the whole great creation. I felt *seen* to the depths of my being and unconditionally loved, despite all my flaws and weaknesses.

I have felt unconditional love welling up from this side, too. The nights I stared at my newborn daughters, fresh from the hands of God, I was transported by a love beyond any boundaries. They came like pure messages straight from the source, telling me I could share in God's joy. To this day, I am always aware that they are treasures, but they are not mine to possess. They are passing gifts on rich paths of their own, who will become more and more independent as they experience their own pains and joys.

The night I strolled through Central Park hand in hand with my new love, we both felt a charge between us so much bigger than any of our expectations. Sure, biology was playing a role, but our love at first sight also vibrated with unsullied newness and the truth of all that we would share. When we were married, I stared up at shafts of light coming into the church through stained-glass windows, and they seemed like a web of protection. Our words of commitment to each other had a sense of union with spirit. I felt that I was vowing to a new life not only with my new husband but with a spirit perfectly placed there to guide me. I felt I was making a contract with God: vowing to attack my genetic patterns and my poor training. That ceremony was one of my first spiritual awakenings. I didn't feel like Cinderella on her way to a life of "happily ever after." I felt like a warrior princess, or Joan of Arc, on a path to self-awareness and truth. I was overwhelmed with love. The trouble was, these transcendent moments were always like bolts of lightning: they came without warning, and when they were gone, I had no idea of where to search for them.

I first started meditating after discovering I was pregnant with Dree. I was reading all kinds of research on how the fetus responds to practically everything in the mother's world, so I assumed that the calming effect of meditation would be beneficial for both of us. I began with a guided meditation called Opening to Receive, which taught me to invite in and receive love and anything else I needed at the time. The music and guidance really helped me get started; on my own, I was not sure what to do. After about a year of working with the tape, I had the confidence to simply meditate with gentle music in the background. That was the same time period when my hatha yoga practice was evolving from Power Yoga workouts to more conscious breath and body movements. Gradually, I discovered that the concentration on breathing during class helped me focus into rewarding meditation if I continued to sit after the active movements were over. Like many others, I learned to begin my sitting practice at the conclusion of my asana practice. It is a natural progression from vigorous movement to stillness and silence.

The next road sign on my path was pointed out by my doctor, Peter Evans. I'd first gone to him looking for ways to cure my fears and my physical exhaustion, but he wasn't making any promises. In fact, at our initial meeting he told me he couldn't see me again for two months. He refused to let me fall into my old pattern and "guruize" him. He simply suggested that I should give up coffee until we met again. I was eager to do whatever he told me, but I was thrown off by his detachment. I had always bound myself to my doctors, needing them to like me. I wanted them to appear to take responsibility for my health. Now, here was a healer who obviously had some deep knowledge, but he certainly wasn't thrusting it forward. This was something new for me. I waited on pins and needles for our next appointment.

When the day finally came for our meeting, I was impressed all over again by his grounded presence. It was just a sense of calmness and wisdom that clung to him. I said that he seemed to be a person who meditates, and when he acknowledged that he did, I asked for instruction. He told me that he wouldn't teach me, but asked if I had read *Autobiography of a Yogi,* the story of the enlightened Indian master Paramahansa Yogananda, who played a leading role in introducing yoga to the West before his death in 1952. I didn't know it at the time, but Dr. Evans is a direct disciple of Yogananda and has been following his teachings for more than fifty years. During this initial discussion, he simply said that if I made a connection with Yogananda's story, I might be interested in the lessons of the

Self-Realization Fellowship, begun by Yogananda and run by his disciples.

To put it bluntly, I was mesmerized by *Autobiography of a Yogi*. I loved the whole great Hindu tradition of spiritual seeking Yogananda grew up in, and I loved the story of his instruction at the feet of various saints. His relationship with his guru, Swami Sri Yukteswar, touched a deep place in me. These were people who knew something I wanted to know about escaping from pain and finding bliss. In no time, I was signed up for the Self-Realization Fellowship lessons, which came in the form of a small package of mail every few weeks. Faced with the first packet, though, I had misgivings. I have always been hesitant about following a specific person in any spiritual matter. In my belief system, I always located God somewhere in nature, and now I had asked a spiritual organization to send me lessons. I could already hear the missionaries and fund-raisers knocking on the door! But to my surprise, nobody ever called to check up on me and nobody ever asked me for money. I was able to simply study the lessons in peace, at my own pace.

At first, I learned the meditation basics I'd been lacking, like how to start and what to focus on. The lessons moved gradually to more esoteric techniques over the next two years. None of the techniques was terribly difficult, but my ability to go deeply inside naturally increased with the time I put into silent practice. The habit of meditative introspection had benefits for other parts of my life as well. I am grateful every day to my husband for all we have learned together. The nuts-and-bolts stuff, the tough times, the moments when I'm repeating my own conditioning are the things that teach me the most. My mother trained me to find fault with men; now I'm learning that the faults I find in others are great indicators of what I should look at in myself. In the heightened awareness of meditation, I can most clearly see my own shortcomings and begin to change.

Yogananda's teachings are deliciously free of dogma. He embraced all love-based spiritual practices and considered all religions and their saints to be meaningful paths to God. All lead to our eventual realization that we are one with God. We start where we are, trying to escape pain and move toward the attainment of bliss. I find meditation a far better way to escape pain than the addictive behavior I had indulged in, and the glimpses of bliss I have are more real than any gift I ever received. It is the only thing I have experienced that always gets better, deeper, and more joyous. My mind still wants to take over, to have important things to say, to make me want things, but I sit regardless, because the more I sit, the more I feel the good stuff. It is always here if I can just get my mind out of the way.

After several years of lessons, I was ready for my initiation into the practice of Kriya yoga, an advanced form of breath control that allows adepts to slow down all the inner functioning of their bodies. The details are kept secret to protect the integrity of the technique as well as out of respect for the great teachers who developed the methods. I'm sure that I will be exploring the technique for the rest of my life. The initiation process involved pledging to accept Paramahansa Yogananda as my guru. As I mentioned, I initially had a problem with the concept of a guru. In my understanding the guru is the only one who actually knows God and can introduce the disciple to God and God realization. In practice, though, devotion to my guru has allowed

me to focus on God more consistently, to better visualize intangible spirit.

When the day came for me to receive my Kriya yoga, I traveled alone to an enormous convention hall in Los Angeles's Bonaventure Hotel. Inside, I found hundreds, maybe thousands of people who were there for the same rite. I began to wonder what on earth I was doing there. People had gathered from all over. Some were gotten up in Birkenstocks and granola wear, while others were elegantly attired and speaking in proper British accents. I felt a bit the way I did at age twelve when I received communion in our small Episcopalian church in Sun Valley. The windows of that church looked up at Mount Baldy, giving me the impression that God was very close by outside. I remember I was in a dress awaiting the unknown initiation into the big adult world of "body of Christ...cup of salvation, blood of Christ." It all sounded a little gruesome to my tender ears.

Finally, people in the convention hall stopped milling around and quietly formed a long line in the largest of the rooms. At the distant head of the line, Self-Realization Fellowship monastics were administering a blessing, and along the way, devotees were placing donations or offerings of flowers and fruit beneath a large photograph of Yogananda's kind face. I waited for an hour at least, slowly making my way toward the unknown ritual. I tried to remain focused on my intention, but I grew tired and began to observe and judge the people around me. I thought that they didn't look especially spiritual. Some even looked angry. I began to imagine leaving, scouting around for the best way out of there. And then I stopped judging and turned my thoughts inward: *Who do you think you are, Mariel?* It was totally

clear to me that I was just one soul among many, all of us looking for ways to find more meaning in our relationships with God. Like the others, I needed help to get out of the pain of my life and feel some bliss.

I took charge of my attitude and remained in the line, and with that decision, the whole experience began to change. As I came closer to the large photograph of Yogananda, the quiet organ music and the conversations around me began to fade into inaudibility. Despite the crowd, I was aware only of his gentle gaze, which seemed directed right at me. I focused all my being on him, and felt such a flood of feeling that I was overwhelmed. I heard only my breath filling and stopping abruptly in my chest when it bumped against my beating heart. Never before had I felt such love as in the embrace of those gentle eyes. He was reassuring me of my protection as a father might reassure a child. I have never been so comforted, so safe, so sure that I was doing the right thing. My love was being returned a hundredfold. Too soon, the line moved forward and I found myself standing before a brilliantly blue-eyed monk who smiled compassionately at my tearstained face. He spoke words of blessing that flowed straight to my heart. I knew that whatever I was to bear in life would be bearable because I had the support of an enlightened master. He is not alive in body, but he is alive in spirit. He was ever-so-present that day.

Since then, I can sometimes sense his unconditional love during my meditation, a love that I watch and allow to transform into the feeling of God's eternal joy. The mental image of my master helps me control the wayward thoughts that want to pull my focus away from bliss. Yogananda

reached enlightenment, or total union with God, in his meditation. I may never have that experience, but with consistent practice I hope to get more and more tastes of the joy that is always new and everlasting. That is why I sit in silence, practicing my Kriya yoga at the beginning and end of each day.

13

FULL WHEEL POSE,
OR *URDHVA DHANURASANA*

I love back bends, and Full Wheel—also
known as Upward Facing Bow—is my favorite. It energizes
my spine by totally compressing and releasing it. From that
powerful action the energy spreads through my whole body.
I feel best if I begin my first Wheel from the simplest
position, lying on my back on the floor, rather than the more
advanced versions, which begin from either a headstand or
a standing position. One step at a time!

So, lying on my back I concentrate on aligning myself
straight on the mat, looking up at the skylights in the ceiling. I next bring my hands up over my head, bending my
elbows so that my palms come down flat on the floor on
either side of my ears. My fingers are spread firmly on the
floor and pointed toward my feet. I feel the earth and see
the sky. Then I bend my knees one at a time, bringing my

feet up close to my butt, spread about as wide as my hips. Breathe. On the exhale I raise my chest and hips, bringing my head back so that the top of it rests on the floor. I make sure that my hands haven't slipped out of position; they are placed so flat on the floor that there is a slight suction at the palms. Continuing to breathe through my nose, on the exhale I press my hands into the floor, straightening my elbows and raising my head and trunk. To arch even higher, I lift my heels and bring my feet closer still to my hands. My chest and upper arms move forward and I can feel my shoulder blades pull down and into my back, their wings almost hidden inside. As I lift my hips and butt, I try to pull my coccyx, sacrum, and lumbar spine away from my waist. In many ways, the move is so subtle that it is more a visualization than a measurable movement.

My spine is totally compressed in this position. On release, there is an exhilarating rush of energy into the spine that lights up my whole body. The head rush is wonderful, too! The feeling I get rising from a major back bend is like a rebirth. Blood and vitality surge through all parts of me. All the fear that comes with being upside down and completely compressed is suddenly released into the atmosphere. I feel purified and complete—tapped into my deepest emotions.

My father went to New York in October 2000 for a heart checkup with some of the best specialists in the country. They diagnosed him as having a weak heart, which was no surprise since he'd had a heart attack in his forties. He had been managing his physical condition, diet, and stress ever since. The experts told him that double bypass surgery could be very beneficial in cases like his. He decided to call me in Los Angeles to ask my opinion.

I was driving on the freeway when my cell phone rang. Hearing his voice and the seriousness of his question, I pulled off the road to give my whole attention to my dad. He wanted to know what I thought of the operation, but I turned his question around and asked him how *he* felt about it. He told me that he wasn't enjoying the quality of his life lately. He could no longer hunt or hike with ease, and tennis and fishing were becoming more difficult by the day. He believed the operation would give him some more truly good years, years of enjoyment. I replied that it sounded as if he knew exactly what he wanted to do and that he should go ahead and do it. He answered that he wanted me to know what was going on—to include me. I was touched that he'd brought me close. We had been so close for many years, but a distance had grown up between us after he remarried, in 1989. He had built a new life with his new partner, and I wasn't so much a part of it.

Angela, his new wife, was an enthusiastic partner who made life exciting for him in ways it had never been with my mother. She brought out Dad's whimsy, and his newfound pleasure made me glad. Angela was never so happy with me or my sisters, though. I suppose it is fairly common for a young wife of an older man to feel herself in a sort of competition with the daughters of her new family. In her defense, Angela had joined a family filled with baggage, as I know only too well.

Angela had originally befriended Muffet, who was living with Dad in the months after our mother's death. Muffet was doing well, painting, cooking for Dad, and taking long walks in the hills with her dogs. Angela was a nice companion, who also took painting lessons from her. Through their friendship, Angela met my father.

At the time, Dad and I were becoming very close again, taking bike rides and hikes together. He revealed a lot of the sadness he felt over the many years of fighting with my mother. I understood—we all regretted not being able to get past so much of Mom's anger, but when a parent or spouse is so ill for such a long time, you simply do what you must to survive. Dad's new life plan, which he'd already begun by selling our family home in Ketchum, was to equip his fishing van with a satellite dish and spend most of his time on the road going from one fabulous fishing stream to the next, listening to classical music and watching sports. He would keep on until it was hunting season in the fall. His home base would be a small condo where Muffet would live full-time.

It seemed like a perfect plan for a man who was most comfortable in a pair of worn-out corduroys or khakis and a faded plaid fishing shirt. He was the perfect outdoorsman, happiest on rich streams wherever he found them around the world. The wilds were his sanctuary. I was delighted that his plan seemed to suit him so well. It was such a humble, almost monastic life he yearned for, giving up the weight and excess of most of life's possessions. I admired him for it. He put it into practice, too, for a few months. He shared with me the joy he felt from his life of ease.

I suppose, though, that he was lonely. Also, he came home from the road to a fragile daughter he had to care for, and that must have weighed on his mind. Whatever the reasons, he quickly gave up his footloose bachelor's life after meeting Angela. She took up fly-fishing so they could spend more time together, and before long they were inseparable. After a short courtship, Dad announced to me at lunch one day that he had asked her to marry him. I was thrilled to see my father so happy. He was like a teenager—a kid in love. So much of his life had been spent just existing in a bad love relationship that it was magic to see him this way. I was pregnant with my second child, and they planned their wedding just two weeks before my due date. It was a fun summer—watching Dad giddy and Muffet excited that her friend was going to marry her daddy. Angela and Jack shared vows in a beautiful outdoor ceremony in Sun Valley in August. Dad looked amazing and so much younger than his sixty five years.

My father the fisherman

After the wedding, Dad's life became progressively more busy and full. He seemed to have little time anymore for his grandchildren, let alone for Muffet. Angela was a busy Mrs. Hemingway, planning parties and organizing new houses. She no longer spent as much time with my sister. All dreams of a quiet, humble fishing life disappeared in a welter of exotic traveling interspersed with visits home to manage the simultaneous construction of a house in Ketchum and a smaller one in the woods of eastern Washington. Muffet was moved into a condominium by herself—very nice, but lonely.

Angela is an interior decorator and she was feverishly achieving the perfect look for each of the new places. The Washington cabin was done in a hunting theme: antler chandeliers and split-log dining furniture carved with scenes of the wild. The Ketchum place seemed to me to have more the feel of a New York apartment. In it, Dad had a perfect room to himself where he could tie flies and read. From simple to elaborate, his lifestyle seemed to be making him very happy.

I saw Dad very rarely for several years, what with all the travel and socializing he was doing. With a new life come new friends and different viewpoints. One surprise for me was seeing Dad metamorphose into a dapper dresser. His pants sported Kelly green and red colors, and everything else was upgraded to match. It wasn't the wardrobe I'd grown up around, but clearly my dad was living another fantasy he must have harbored. He was almost like an English gentleman. What made him familiar to me was his ever-present love of the outdoors; never mind if he was spending the evening in velvet slippers and a silky smoking jacket, he still knew that the brown trout in the Little Wood River would be biting at five the next morning.

Angela took care of him laboriously, and I think he needed it. After spending so much of his life taking care of a sick partner who was angry with him, he deserved to be pampered. It made me sad, though, that my family got to spend so little time with him. He had so much knowledge that I would have liked my girls to be exposed to. He was the man who shared his love of the outdoors with me. He gave me a sense of awe and wonder in the direct meeting with nature—something I hoped I could pass on to my kids in the same way. Muffet, too, became sad to lose contact with Dad. Soon the loneliness of her life led her to leave Ketchum and move to a larger town where she could share an apartment with other fragile souls. She continues to this day in the same place, making her art and cooking for her housemates.

All this preamble is to explain why it was a big deal for me when Dad called to discuss his decision about the impending heart surgery. I was worried about him, but I was happy to be included in his life again. We continued our discussion over several days, and when he decided to go ahead with the operation I promised to fly back east to visit him in the hospital. He told me the visit was not at all necessary, but I knew in my heart that I needed to be there for my own sake, if not for his.

The double bypass surgery went very well. When I spoke with his doctor, he said Dad was one of the strongest patients he'd had in a long time. Dad sounded so vibrant when he called me from recovery! He reiterated that I didn't need to come see him—that he was fine—but something about his voice worried me. So I took the red-eye to New York, arriving at 5:50 A.M. and dragging my burned-out self to Angela and Jack's apartment. Angela was completely preoccupied about Dad. She called the hospital and yelled at the nurses, admonishing them to take better care of him. We family members may have thought she had an odd style of influence on Dad, but nobody could say she didn't love or care for him. By seven-thirty in the morning, we were off to the hospital.

Dad was chipper and he looked great. He had color in his face and a full cackle in his laugh. As he told us stories, Angela became distressed on hearing that he'd had trouble getting a nurse's attention in the middle of the night. He was just recounting the experience, not complaining about it, but Angela took it as a call to action. Clearly, heads were going to roll. She went off to settle somebody's hash, leaving us together to chitchat. It was nice to be alone with him. It had been a long time. He spoke in a florid manner about the results of the presidential election (the Bush-Gore results were still in dispute in Florida). He was pissed off that they hadn't declared Bush the president, and I wasn't about to declare my more Democratic opinion. It struck me how funny it is that the way we're brought up doesn't always determine our eventual political beliefs as adults. So, I listened to Daddy's rant with a smile on my face, thinking in the back of my mind of the many fishing trips we'd taken together when I was a child. We saw rivers and streams all over Idaho, Oregon, and Montana. I was never very good at fly-fishing, but we both loved the quiet solitude. I can still feel the cold, crisp water and the bite of early-morning frost even in summer. I had a picture in my head of him casting for steelhead in the current of the Umpqua River, could feel the hush of his intention and the focus of his eyes on the water. The whole of my recollection was wrapped in the feeling of peace that enveloped his soul out there.

A nurse entered the room, breaking our reverie. She took Dad's blood pressure, remarking that it was a bit high. "You must be excited that your daughter is here," she said, and left. Suddenly, Dad changed from our ice-breaking chatter and looked directly into my eyes. "I'm not scared anymore. I know Angela's frightened, but I'm not. Whatever is going to happen, it'll be OK. I'm OK with it."

I found it strange that he was telling me this now. He had already survived the worst part. The operation was a success, and here he was talking as though it hadn't happened yet. I said, "Well, you're doing so well, Daddy, and you look great. It will be wonderful to get outside again." And as I said those words, Dad began to wheeze. He seemed to be choking. In a panic, I asked him, "Daddy, are you choking? Do you need help?" Clearly he did. Something was terribly wrong and he wasn't able to answer me. His body began to contort, convulsing. "Daddy, Daddy, what's wrong?" I watched his eyes roll back into his head and I knew in that moment that he was gone. It was as if I watched his spirit flee his body. I could feel his presence in the room, but not in his body. Finally, I came to myself enough to jump up and run into the hall screaming for help.

Within seconds, a team of surgeons, who coincidentally were in the corridor, piled into his room. I watched them begin desperate measures to revive my father. They ripped his gown off and it wasn't long before they were opening his chest. Nobody realized I was still in the room, standing quietly in the corner watching the whole mind-blowing procedure. They actually opened his chest right there in the room. It was beyond surreal. His body was no longer human—he was a specimen. He was science, and for me it was science fiction. I felt Dad's presence right there next to me, watching too. We both knew his body was suffering, but his soul had retreated to a safer place. I was finally discovered and whisked out of there by an incredulous nurse. She took me to the nurses' station, where I sat for at least an hour in shock.

Eventually, one of Dad's heart specialists showed up to talk with me. He said that from what he could tell at that point, one of the sutures from the bypass had burst. It is a rare occurrence, but sometimes it happens. Apparently, my arrival had caused a surge in his blood pressure—which led me to wonder for weeks if it was all my fault. I guess it might have been, but other things can cause blood pressure to go up as well. As my head cleared, I remembered that I had to get hold of Angela, who soon arrived on the floor in a total panic. Sobbing, she demanded information and understanding from everybody in the area. She was a widow and I knew it, but she wasn't going to settle there easily. She was terrified. I watched her trying to control the situation; for three weeks after, while Dad lay brain-dead in a coma, I watched her trying to make him come back into his body.

The atmosphere was so bizarre that I found myself devoting my daily visits to his bedside, as well as the hours in a tiny, windowless waiting room, to simply observing. I did nothing but watch. Watch and listen. Angela, in tears, read hope into the doctor's every word. She was writing in her head the outcome she wanted. The more the discouraging evidence piled up, the more distraught she became. She ate nothing and nervously applied and reapplied makeup. I could see her trying to paint on a happy face. She wanted everything that had happened to be undone, and the more she fought the present moment, the more pain she was in.

I thought of Dad as no longer connected to that body, but as a spirit making amends for his life. Quietly, so that others couldn't hear me, I whispered into his ear how much I loved him. "Daddy, I know that you're going. It's all right for you to go. We will miss you terribly, but we'll survive. We will all be OK. I just want you to know how much I love you, and Stephen loves you, too. Dree and Langley love you so much. Margaux had a difficult life, but it wasn't your fault. She loved you like crazy. And so does Muffet. You have been a great father to all of us. You were a wonderful husband to Mom. You were so loyal and true to her despite everything. You have been a great man and your life has been a good one. You can put it all down now. You don't have to hang on to this wrecked body for us. We understand."

Every day for several weeks I repeated these words to him. Sometimes I was choked with tears because his eyes would suddenly open and look around blankly. It was agonizing to see him looking physically alive, yet know that he wasn't really there. He was so vulnerable, lying there full of tubes, immobile as he had never been in life. I wondered why he wouldn't just go. Meanwhile, the doctors were awaiting the results of a final brain scan to see if there was anything going on in his head, or if it was just the life-support machines keeping his thoughtless body alive.

It was a powerful time for me. My daily round of quiet talk was closing wounds in me in a way that felt very meaningful. I had the feeling his spirit was afraid at some level, and that this time I spent expressing previously unspoken sentiments was healing and completing our relationship. I spoke for Margaux and Muffet because I was the only one able to.

I felt very alone walking the eight long blocks from the hospital to my rooms between Park and Madison. I didn't feel lonely—just alone. I was becoming an orphan. The bonds to my parents were going. It felt as if I was separating not only from my father but from my mother as well. In my friend's borrowed apartment, I cried deeply for Margaux, too. Dad's death seemed to bring out buried emotions for all the loved ones I had lost. When Mother died, I remember being unable to feel enough. After Margaux's death I felt an enormous amount of fear, but never the mourning—the sense of loss over permanent physical separation from somebody I had loved so much I had a hard time separating her existence from mine. My confusion over our identities had clouded my grief. Now, with Dad there was no confusion about our relationship. He was a decent man, a good father, and a loyal companion. I could let go of him knowing he had always done his best with me— with us all. In letting him go, I was able to release Mother and Margaux, too.

I cried tears for them all, tears that came from a place I didn't know could be reached. It felt as though a hard rock deep inside me was being squeezed and squeezed. Eventually the constant pressure burst the hard place open, flooding my body with emotional catharsis. A rushing of cool

and soothing water became a force of current that I couldn't
stand up against or escape. The temperature of the relentless
flow became so cold it hurt. As I finished my heaving sobs,
I felt as if I had just come out of an icy lake—shivering
cold, numb and tingly. I felt better for having gone through
it even though I wasn't sure I could handle it while it was
actually happening.

Stephen and the girls came east to visit me over Thanksgiving. We all knew that the life-support machines would
be turned off soon, but Angela needed a little more time
with Dad. Fair enough—losing a spouse is a huge deal. I
couldn't stay in New York very much longer, so I planned
my last visit to the hospital a few days after Thanksgiving.
I wanted Stephen and the girls near me when I said those
final good-byes to Dad. We weren't sure if it would be good
for the girls to see their grandpa in such a state, but we
hoped it might give them a sense of closure. I was very
worried that they might freak out, seeing him so full of
tubes, especially if his eyes opened while they were there.
The best plan we could come up with was to give them
plenty of support and an easy exit if they were afraid. As
it turned out, we needn't have worried. It was fascinating
to watch them when they entered his room. Dree thought
he looked great and peaceful. She said, "He looks good,
Mommy. And he's not afraid anymore. You can see it in
his eyes." She liked touching him and she spoke quietly
to him as I had been doing, telling him that she loved
him and that it is beautiful where he was going. She was
nearly thirteen and ever so wise. Langley looked on quietly
and put her hand on his while looking for my approval. I
told her she was fine, and she seemed relieved to feel his

Cool girls on the subway in New York City

warm skin. She just stood looking solemnly at him, saying nothing.

I told the three of them it was time to say good-bye, and I began my final round of love and reassurance to my dad. Dree put her hand on my back and her other hand on Dad's forehead. Langley hugged me from behind, saying, "Mommy, don't cry. He's already OK." I told her I knew that; they were just tears that had to come. She kissed the small of my back. Stephen wrapped his arms around all of us while we silently prayed. At the end, I asked Stephen to take the girls out so I could meditate next to him. I wanted to regain some composure and find peace with him. They left me sitting silently by his side, the only movement the streaming of tears down my cheeks. When I was done I said, "Good-bye, Daddy. I do love you so..."

For the next four or five days it was his wife's time, and I hope she made her peace with his passing, too. On December 1, he was taken off life support in the late afternoon. At 9 P.M. that evening in Los Angeles I was enjoying a deep, peaceful meditation. I had been seeing my father in my mind's eye with a huge smile on his face. He was wearing his fishing clothes with no shoes. He began laughing just as the phone rang. It was Angela telling me that Daddy was gone. I cried again and Stephen held me sweetly—like I was a little girl. The girls came in and held me on our bed until I fell asleep in all their arms.

The bittersweet, fragile process of mourning for my family didn't play out in the focused way I imagined as I fell asleep that evening. Two memorial services were planned, one in New York and another in Sun Valley right after Christmas. But just as I sat down to collect my thoughts about Dad, Stephen was diagnosed with a lethal form of cancer. This sudden new development jumped onto center stage and overwhelmed me. So instead of feeling my deep connection to Dad while eulogizing him, my mind was being pulled in a hundred directions, thinking about surgeries, biopsies, and how to hold my little family together.

During the living of those days, everything took more flexibility, patience, and faith than I'd expected, but that seems to be the way of life. So here I am, up in *Urdhva Dhanurasana* at the height of my Upward Facing Bow. My body is boldly reaching for the heavens in the front, my feet solidly grounded in the earth, and my back compressed in subservience to the powerful expression. Finishing, I bring myself back to a standing position and feel a surge of equilibrium finding its way back to me. It is a hope giver— practice and reassurance for the difficult process of finding my balance again after the death of my father.

in memory of jack hemingway

My father, in an unconventional way, was a sort of priest. Although he did not preach in a specific church or belong to a specific denomination, he did praise God every day. His faith was private, yet vast in its beauty.

He communed with God in the greatest cathedral of all: nature. The walls of his church were made up of the sage-brushed hills of Idaho or Washington, or the banks of trout streams everywhere. The hills swelled with the cooing of doves, the flush of chukars, and the screech of a hawk. These birds made up his choir.

His communion took place in the infinitude of streams he fished and waded. Daddy felt those waters against his solid legs, he felt the cold flow and the current, and in those moments he was one with spirit. Those were his uninterrupted hours of prayer and meditation with the creatures and places he loved the most. He was with his flock, in his church.

The peace that Daddy felt in the outdoors was a gift from God, and in return he gave back through tireless efforts to preserve the wilderness and its waters. He was a humble and grateful man. He was also immensely generous, for he gave me that same love of life and its subtle outdoor mysteries. For that I am thankful beyond words. I can only hope that I will pass it along to my own two daughters.

Although my father's sermon here on earth is done, I know that he continues to climb heavenly hills and wade in sacred waters. He is smiling that Jack Hemingway smile and chuckling to himself, realizing that he really did know this bliss after all. He was a wonderful, loving father, grandfather, and man. I miss him.

CORPSE POSE,
OR SAVASANA

Ending a session of hatha yoga properly is essential. To rest and quiet the body is so rewarding, and yet often it is difficult. After all the carefully controlled movement, it is hard to let go and surrender into the earth. I begin by leaning back on my elbows with my legs extended in front of me, checking that my trunk and legs are lined up straight. As I lie on the floor, I lower my back, vertebra by vertebra, making sure everything is lengthened before relaxing. My head is straight, my neck long, and I concentrate on finding ease in my throat. I bring my shoulder blades in to open my chest. All along my body I can feel myself sinking into the floor. My sacrum is placed down evenly, my arms and legs symmetrical and my fingers curling naturally. I make any adjustments needed and then gradually lie still as a corpse.

I have practiced, sweated, and been acutely aware of the movements of my body. I have been trying to watch the constant flux of my thinking mind without getting dragged into the process. Now it is time to let it all go. Let the practice go. Let the muscles go. Let my intention and my mind go. Surrender.

Surrender is far more than just a little mini vacation I give myself. Like the deaths we deal with—of habit, youth, changing friendships, joys gone by, our loved ones—life is the practice of surrender. My life is constantly guiding me to learn to give in to what is happening around me, to accept my circumstances, accept my choices, and especially to surrender to the shocks life deals me. On December 1, 2000, my father was taken off a variety of life-support machines after a few weeks in a coma in a New York hospital. I knew he had already left his body because I saw him go shortly before, as I sat watching him. He simply was not there anymore.

My mind began probing the huge gulf his leaving had opened up. At first, I was holding it together, but I began to feel surrounded by the surreal energy of his actual death. I bumped into the strange and inescapable fact that I was now an orphan. It began to dawn on me that my bond with my father was much stronger than I had suspected; that was a painful surprise to be surrendered to. His leaving also brought the deaths of my mother and sister back in fresh and painful ways. This was going to be a much bigger and sadder process than I had realized while I was sitting by his bedside.

Meanwhile, the routines of life were not stopping to wait for me. Stephen, who was taking care of the kids in Los Angeles, had an annoying mole removed from the top of his

Stephen with Dree and Langley

head. On December 5, the dermatologist asked him to come to the office, to learn that he had a malignant melanoma in stage five of development—the worst scenario imagin able. Stephen was frightened. He had a longtime obsession with melanomas and always mentioned how fast they killed you. He saw himself dead in a few weeks. I was beyond shocked. My only reaction, once I could react, was denial. It made no sense. Just as on the day I fell in love with him, I was submerged in water, unable to understand his words but acutely aware of his body and face. I saw the gentle ness and lines his still-youthful face had acquired over our years together. His usually bottomless brown eyes showed no more dreams or depth, but a window opening to a wall of misunderstanding. I longed to hold him the way I had the first day I touched him, but he seemed to have left his body the way my father had just days before. Occasionally, I was able to emerge from my fluid haven to hear him promising to teach me in the next few weeks how to run his film company. That would send me back to watching him from underwater.

Dree was angry and unable to accept what was happening. Langley was terrified and crying. The reality of their reactions pulled me into the present and into mommy mode. "Daddy is just shocked and afraid—it's going to be all right—we just need to figure out how to deal with it." I took the first step, and then the next. Consoling and distracting them, I managed to get them into their rooms doing their homework. *Routine.* My mind kept chanting, *Routine,* and *Breathe. This surely will not be easy.* Cancer is a nefarious guest, and one I thought I had willed away after my mother's long fight. My dad had just died. Wasn't that what we were dealing with now? I guessed not, so I pulled on a nurturing cloak, hoping I could hide my own fears over Stephen's condition and control my need to cry for my father and my sister and my mother. I had subconsciously postponed mourning for them until Dad's death. I must have assumed that a volcanic eruption of feeling would be better or easier than trailing it out over time. I obviously wasn't banking on any other family tragedy to get in the way; but with Stephen ill there was no time for my feelings of loss.

After several hours of calls with our doctor, we were led to the John Wayne Cancer Institute, in Santa Monica. It was not an easy venture to get placed in one of the most renowned cancer treatment hospitals in the country. I used my name unabashedly, pleading and manipulating to get my husband scheduled for surgery within the next few days. Stephen and I met Dr. Eddy Hsueh, the leader of the team of physicians working on his case. He wasn't able to offer us much hope, but we nodded at everything he said, secretly hanging our hats on every slightly optimistic statistic. Then he closed by giving us the frightening odds against being able to get every single cancer cell when the tumor was surgically removed from the top of Stephen's head. Any of those strange cells left behind would share the propensity of all melanoma cells to metastasize wildly, spreading the cancer throughout his body.

I thought I could hardly be more scared until I looked at Stephen and realized that he was completely undone. All he could imagine was the certainty that his daughters would be left without a father, that he would be forced to abandon us. He had always felt that he was here to protect me, whether I needed it or not, and he felt that way doubly about his young, innocent daughters. Now, with practically no warning, all that was crumbling and coming out backward.

Somehow, though, I didn't slip into complete panic; instead, I began to feel the terror of what we were hearing become my life's new reality. The denial fell away from me. In that cold light, the sense of security I felt with my guru and my spiritual practice came to my rescue. There was no fighting these circumstances; that much was clear. The thought came to me that crisis has a way of empowering us. I thought that Stephen would have his best chance of getting well if he used this drama as a goad to search deeply inside, discovering, among other things, the role emotions were playing in his illness. For my part, I saw this as a challenge to return to a situation much like my past; this time taking it to a place of acceptance and learning, rather than fear and denial.

When my mother became ill, I refused it. I placed a heavy burden on myself to keep her cancer at bay. I lived in unrelenting fear. She had to live for me, and it was my job to push her death away. Now, at thirty-nine, I could see that I was no more in control of my husband's cancer than a stranger's on the street. It wasn't mine and there was no willing it away. All the guidance I got in my meditation was to love Stephen and provide for him what I was able to do. I prepared the hundreds of vitamins he took daily, cooked the special foods he needed, and held our little family together as well as I could. I would learn to be patient, supportive, and accepting.

Stephen's homeopathic doctor immediately put him on a heavy regimen of vitamins and prescribed a diet exactly like the one I had been advised to follow a few months before. So he joined me for the first time in all my dietary experimenting, both of us eating wholly organic foods that were high in protein and good fats and extremely low in sugars and the carbohydrates that turn quickly to sugar in the body. The idea was to deny the cancer cells the sugar they need to multiply at top speed.

Unlike me, Stephen is a sugar addict. He lived on cookies, bread, pasta, french fries, and Coca-Cola. When he heard that his chances of survival were 35 to 40 percent, though, he lay prostrate at our doctor's feet asking to be shown how to eat this way. Since I knew the diet and was a certified food fascist with myself, I was assigned the task of making Stephen understand his new food program and keeping him in line. I thought it would be a tough assignment. After all, this was a man who didn't see the difference between a doughnut and an apple because they are both the same size. But I hadn't reckoned on the power that the terror of death can exert on a dieter. When Stephen made his commitment, he never faltered from the eating program. To this day he is a poster boy for healthy eating and snacking. He eats eggs and nuts and—God bless this man who never let a steamed vegetable cross his plate, let alone his lips— he now eats broccoli, cauliflower, and spinach.

The surgery was hugely successful and surprisingly more crucial than had been anticipated. Dr. Hsueh removed a much bigger and deeper tumor than anybody had visualized. It touched the bone, which made it an extra dangerous proposition. During the surgery, the lymph nodes at the sides of Stephen's neck were removed because metastasized cancer cells were almost certain to be piling up there from a tumor as large and well developed as the one on his head.

Waiting around the hospital for Stephen to come out of the anesthesia and for the biopsies on the lymph nodes to come back from the lab gradually became surreal for me. Stephen's brother Eric and I were prowling around the cafeteria trying to find a healthy protein snack to eat, but everything was low-fat muffins, cereal, or skim-milk breads and pastas. You would think that heart disease was the only killer in America. Every one of the foods available was either flat-out sugar or a carbohydrate that became sugar almost as soon as it was eaten. *Anybody ever heard of diabetes around here?* Next to me on the wall was the kind of diet poster I was familiar with from elementary school. It was designed to promote healthy eating, but all the recommended foods were breads, grains, fruits, and pasta—what I thought of as the sugar group. The poster acknowledged our need for protein, but only in small amounts, and fats were practically banned as poison. In my overemotional state I could practically see the cancer cells dividing and growing in the rich sugar medium flowing through the collective bloodstream. I felt like screaming, *We are in a hospital, people. This diet chart may be what's killing us.* I probably felt guilty in some way about failing to fix Stephen's diet long ago.

My mind raced off on a rant; I started thinking of some of my daughters' sweet friends who are hugely overweight. I often ask what they eat and am told, "Oh, my mom has me on a low-fat diet. We've tried everything." They begin their day on cereal and fruit with nonfat milk—three sugars, thank you. Lunch is pizza if they eat at all, and dinner is pasta, bread (without butter, of course), and maybe a salad. Not to mention that children live on diet drinks, which are nothing but chemicals. It all began to merge into a fury in my head. *Our children are being raised on poison, and the AMA is doing nothing to straighten them out!* I was ready to start breaking things right there in the hospital. *OK, Mariel, calm down. You can't fix anybody but yourself, so maybe focus again on providing some good choices for your own family.* It took an effort of will to let it go.

I returned to the waiting room where there were fewer incitements to riot. Eric and I sat glumly together while the last hour of waiting crawled by. Finally we were told that Stephen was regaining consciousness, and we were led to his room. It is always a shock to see somebody who has gone through an operation. His head was bandaged like a sheik's, with a fold under his chin. His face had an upsetting gray pallor, to be kind about it, and he looked much older than his fifty-one years—and he had never even looked forty-five before. He was clearly in pain, but wanted to go right home. The ride was nearly unbearable for me and pure torture for Stephen. Any turn or change of speed for a stop-light nauseated him. I tried to be gentle, but the Los Angeles traffic makes its own demands. In the back of my mind, I kept visualizing the turns of Malibu Canyon looming ahead of us. I ached for him as he gripped the armrest all through the twisting sections of the road.

When we got home, I was shot into my past, helping my ever-so-sick mother from the car and into her bedroom and then on to the bathroom to vomit. Stephen did the same things. The difference was that, unlike my mother, he didn't want me near. And most important, I knew that he is a fighter who would do everything possible to slay whatever dragon was uncoiling inside him. My mother, on the other hand, never challenged her own part in her cancer—her grief, her fear, and her resentment. Whether right or wrong, she always just passively accepted it as an outside force, a terrible accident. Stephen was prepared to change every-thing about his life to get well.

His recovery from the surgery was painful and arduous. His head remained wrapped for weeks, all through the holidays. The news from the doctors was good, though. They said they were very surprised and happy to learn that no cancerous cells were found in the lymph nodes removed from Stephen's neck. We began to hope that the tumor hadn't metastasized in some big way. Now the main thing to do was get on with the recovery. Get on the diet, take the vitamins, and endure the CAT scans and MRIs with their heavy doses of radiation. Melanomas do not respond to either treatment radiation or chemotherapy, which is part of the reason that advanced skin cancers of this type are so deadly. The scans were aimed at detecting any new tumors at the earliest possible stage. Our low-sugar diet was aimed at starving any cancer cells that were still in his system, so that new tumors would be found growing slowly at the petite sixty-thousand-cell stage rather than rioting at the six-hundred-thousand-cell disaster stage. The vitamins were to give his body every possible advantage in dealing with these rogue cells that had forgotten all restraint.

Throughout it all, I could see Stephen exploring deep inside to get at the sources of his emotional pain. He was distant, and rightly so. My role was just to watch, providing meals, supplements, and a shoulder to lean on when he wanted it. I was waiting in case he felt safe to talk with me. It was a real challenge to stay out of it: to nurture, not control; to mother the girls and take care of myself. I was greatly helped by my daily hatha yoga practice, followed by sitting in silent meditation—*surrender, surrender, surrender.* I worked to surrender to what was happening now and to understand my own feelings of fear from the past. I accepted, more or less successfully, that this was all beyond my control.

Stephen endured repeated treatments with an experimental new melanoma vaccine that had to be injected by means of scores of large needles poked into his groin and trunk. The wounds oozed for weeks and he began referring to me as the Bride of Stephenstein. It was grim humor, but in my book any humor in a situation like that is a good

Our family Christmas photo, 1998

sign. And indeed, a year and a half has passed since his
terrifying diagnosis. The continuous MRIs and CAT scans
have not detected a single new cancer cell. He still follows
his diet, works with a fantastic therapist, and meditates daily.
They say that you are not out of the woods until you have
cleared five years cancer-free, but we are feeling optimistic.
Stephen is consistent about avoiding stress, a change that
goes pretty deep into his attitude toward life. As a result,
we are benefiting as a family. I am learning to observe him
instead of trying to fix him. I believe I healed some of the
pain of illness that I have carried with me since puberty. I
learned again that to care for my family, I must first care
for myself. Corpse pose is the complete relaxation that pre-
pares me for meditation, and meditation is the best form
of personal grounding and rejuvenation I have discovered.
It has come to me as a gift that all my yoga practice was
leading to—a gift of peace and bliss that enables me to
face all the dramas as my best self.

15

EAGLE POSE,

OR *GARUDASANA*

Eagle pose is a balancing posture with the arms and legs intricately entwined. It is always an interesting pose for me, one I like to do whenever I feel the need to break up my usual yoga routine. It requires some flexibility, a lot of trust, and most of all, balance. In the instant after I've swung my arms and legs into position, I'm fascinated to see whether I'm going to be able to balance or if I will be falling over. It's a good reality check on the day.

Today I prepare by standing at the head of my mat looking out the window at the fast-moving clouds, white against the bright blue mountain sky. Coming to the studio, I was whipped by the wind, and these clouds are moving so fast that I feel off balance just looking at them. I need to find a focus point that is more stable, something right for today. I don't want the world moving out from under me right now. So the mat and focus are reoriented toward one of my beloved hills, and I find my solid base in *Tadasana*. Bending my legs slightly, I place my hands on my hips and focus again. Then I raise my right leg and find a stable balance on the left. Exhaling deeply, I cross the right thigh and knee over the left, taking the right shin behind my left calf. The toes of my right foot peek out around the inside of my left shin. It sounds complicated, and the balance is hard, but basically my right leg is just twisted counterclockwise around my left, about as tightly as it can go. On days when I feel supple, it is fairly easy; other days, my legs feel shorter than normal.

Now, mirroring the way the right leg wrapped around the left, I wrap my left arm around my right. It goes like this: Inhaling, I raise my hands in front of my face, palms facing each other. On the exhale, I swing my left elbow over the right, fitting the left elbow into the crook of the right. Smoothly continuing to twine my arms, I bring my right hand toward my face and my left away, ending with my hands crossed, the fingers of the right hand on the left palm—a human pretzel resisting the tendency to fall over to the right. Once I'm firmly on my foot again I stretch my "wings" up toward the sky, away from my center. My elbows lift to shoulder level as I continue my slight squat. The left knee wants to splay out, but I don't let it go. Then the lift is followed by a contraction, as I pull my elbows toward my breast and belly, into my center. My back rounds and I exhale. It is as if everything has become small. I should be feeling light, birdlike, ready to re-create the pose on my right leg. Instead I feel only off center. I cannot balance or focus or find peace. I'm wavering, feeling more like a bird shot out of the sky than like an eagle.

In November of 2001, I bundled up our little Crisman-Hemingway clan and headed to the island of Kauai for a combined celebration of Thanksgiving and my fortieth birthday. I had considered different birthday scenarios for the big four-oh. The day seemed important beyond the mere turning of a calendar page. Somehow, I felt this birthday represented a subtle transition in my lifelong quest to understand myself. Rather than trying to figure out who I am, I am learning to accept the person that I now understand myself to be. It only makes sense, now that a serious chunk of my time is in the rearview mirror. And I'm beginning to feel that I have some things to show for my efforts. I have finally found a way to eat that suits me. My hatha yoga exercises my body, heart, and mind, and it isn't an overstatement to say that I love the practice. My dependence on acting as a means of self-definition has diminished. I don't seem to need the public acclaim so much in order to understand who I am. I no longer feel a helpless victim of my family's strange interactions and flawed genetic pool. I'm surprised to find that just being Mariel is all right by me, and my praise is finally coming from inside myself. I have become a woman, a mother, a wife, and above all, a yogini devoted to God and my guru.

This new comfort with who I am also seems to give me a significant ability to accept what life has in store for me. I like the phrase "I accept what God puts on my plate each and every day." So going out and seeking excitement on my birthday seemed to be the antithesis of contemplating and celebrating the growth of my life. I wanted solitude,

My happiest role

family, warmth, a gentle breeze, and the ocean. Kauai became
the gift I wanted most.

The view from our little house was exactly what I had
fantasized about. We looked down from a hill on a perfect
private cove surrounded by low hills. A little stretch of sandy

beach was joined on both sides by encircling volcanic rocks that ran out to the headlands. Inside the protecting coral reef, the water was shallow and inviting, and outside, gigantic breakers were smashing beautifully and terribly into the rocks: some of the largest of the year, we heard later. The whole scene acted on the four of us like a magnet, drawing us down the red dirt path through the noni bushes and palms, past the feral chickens, to the beach.

We couldn't wait to try the water, so we dragged three plastic sea kayaks from under the bushes down to the water's edge. There were life vests for Dree and Langley, who would share a boat, but none for Stephen or me. No worries, the water was shallow and both of us are strong swimmers. The girls dragged paddles into their kayak and pushed off. Stephen and I looked at them proudly and then promptly shoved our boats off into the gentle surf. The sight of the crashing waves in the distance was exhilarating and chilling at the same time.

"I hear there are huge turtles out past the reef," I shouted to the girls. "Tomorrow, when the waves are smaller, we can look for them." The sun glinted on the water, the wind flowed over me—I felt that the vacation was beginning for real. In my happy, dreamy state, I suddenly noticed that the shallow bottom was moving by quickly underneath me. The cove was much more turbulent than it had looked from shore or from the safe vantage of the house up on the hill. I looked up to check on everybody and saw that the girls were caught in a strong current, heading rapidly to the right and toward deeper water along the shore. Langley screamed as their boat crashed into the rocks. They lost their paddles on the impact, and the next swell shoved them along, closer to where the really huge waves were hitting the jagged lava flow. They were obviously too panicked to help themselves out of a situation that was getting more dangerous by the second.

I started madly paddling toward them, oblivious to my own danger in the same currents that had trapped them. Stephen, who had not been spaced out, was ahead of me, reaching the girls within seconds. He fell from his kayak in the surf, but helped the girls out of their boat and up to safety on the shore. Hugely relieved, I relaxed for a second and saw Stephen's hat floating away in the current. He had lost it in his dunking. I imagined his poor, melanoma-scarred head exposed to the tropical sun and made a snap decision to get the hat. Just a few strokes after the hat and my plan began to seem like a bad one. The damned thing seemed to be swimming quickly toward the rocks. My mind started into overdrive, and all the thoughts were negative. *I don't feel stable in this kayak. I'm not used to doing something physical where my legs lie outstretched, useless. All the control has to come from my arms, which are not used to holding a paddle.*

The hat, passive on the flowing water, naturally drew me right into the worst of the current. The bottom dropped away as I begin to get into much bigger surf. The boat was caught on a turbulent eddy line between the currents, with waves coming from both sides. I put the paddle deeply into the water, fighting for control, and the current swept it in under the side of the boat. I had to let go or the paddle itself would lever me upside down; the loss of it left me with no means of control at all. The next big wave toppled me overboard, and the boat vanished in the foaming chaos.

My instinct was to turn toward shore and fight the current with everything I had. That was the way to shallow water, safety, and my family. I tried to power my way through, but each time I lifted my gasping head, they were farther away. I was going backward! Everything around me was getting more violent as the return flow from the whole cove pushed me to meet the massive swells coming in from thousands of miles of open ocean. The whole maelstrom was crashing into the rocks, and I was riding helplessly right into the center of it. I no longer even had a remote sense of the bottom somewhere down there below my feet. The waves began to break on me, catching me first in their acceleration toward shore and then dragging me back with the outwash. I had no idea of how to handle this water with its shocking weight. I lost all notion of where the surface was, and that tipped me over into helpless panic. When I tumbled to the surface, waves that looked far off were suddenly breaking on top of me, cutting off my desperate breath of salty splash and my cry for help. My last view was of Stephen on the shore looking back at me. Down again in the dark, violent undertow, I was pulled apart in every direction—my legs dragged sideways while my arms and torso were pulled upside down and around— a helpless rag doll.

My mind started to think about my situation. *Where am I? How come I can't swim in this? What can I do?* And right in the flow of thoughts came a real stopper—*I'm going to drown.* With that realization, I was completely overcome by terror. My eyes bulged, as if seeing something in the murk would help me. The awful images and ideas totally ran away with me—*I'm going to die and I'm so not ready for this!* With all my spiritual training and seeming acceptance of death, I was no more ready to die than to fly. I could make no connection with my guru or with God. I was alone in fighting the ocean. That struck me as a tremendously pathetic reaction. When next the waves pushed me to the surface, I couldn't see Stephen or even locate the shore. It was the end of hope. *I can't do this—I can't do this—I can't fight this*—and in feeling my hopelessness I was suddenly suspended in time. *No,* I thought, *I cannot fight this. My panic is not working for me.*

Beneath the water again, yet now above the experience somehow, I could clearly see that I was drowning. It seemed all right. My frantic self was finally exhausted, and I became intensely aware of the presence of God and my guru. Surrender was possible with that awareness, and I succumbed to whatever was meant to be. I still didn't like the idea of drowning, but it now seemed thinkable. I was scared, but peaceful. My body was still swimming, only now without fighting my situation. I caught breaths when I could between the waves. Any lifeguard could have told me that I was starting to do the right thing, but there was none around. All I could think to do was pray. Clasping the Kriya band on my right arm that helps deepen my connection with my guru, I began a mental prayer. *Please, God and Master, bring me in safely or take me out peacefully—I am yours, God, alone.* I thought these words over and over, and with each repetition I felt calmer. The ocean was still raging, but I was no longer its victim. The waves and currents fought over me, but I wasn't resisting.

For a long period there was quiet. My world became soundless until my feeling of release was suddenly broken by a shocking collision with a rock. I grabbed the jagged surface, trying to embrace it with both arms and legs. The noise and power of the next breaker surged all through me, lifting and scraping the full length of my body on top of the boulder. Like an octopus, I sucked the rock with my legs; my fingernails dug through the weeds and shells to find a grip for my hands. Looking up, I saw that I was near the shore.

The girls were a hundred yards off to my right, frantic and crying, but they weren't running to me as I might have expected. Dree was clapping her hands in agony. Then I realized that I couldn't see Stephen. "Where is Daddy?" I shouted. Through her sobs, Dree answered, "He went in for you." My heart fell out of me knowing what danger he had entered to save me. Adrenaline poured through me, enabling me to rise from my precarious perch in the surf and dash through the foam, leaping from rock to rock as though I wore boots. On reaching the girls, I began to scan the water desperately, but I couldn't see anything. Dree was screaming, but even more awful was Langley's silent stare, her big eyes sending two lines of tears down her face. "Stop it, baby," I said to Dree. "Screaming isn't going to help Daddy. We've got to pray. Focus all your energy on getting Daddy in." At that moment, Stephen's face emerged from the water, all gray. His eyes were distraught. I could hear Langley chanting by my side, "Mommy, Daddy, God, Master, please!" over and over again. Dree was silent now, and focused, her eyes on her father like a lighthouse calling him home.

Another huge wave buried him for what seemed like too long. When he came up in the frothy aftermath he looked distant. He was looking at us, but he couldn't make a connection. He was focused inward on his struggle to prevent the ocean from taking him. I was crying freely, praying. Why did I call for his help when he couldn't save me? I knew standing there that I couldn't possibly save him. I was filled with the thought that the girls were going to watch their daddy drown and that I was going to watch my husband die. *Dear Lord, we've been tackling cancer, and now he's going out with the force of nature. I will lose my partner and my love. This is the man I thought I chose forever.* My own experience in that water had just taught me that acceptance and surrender were my only choices. I told myself, *Pray—love him and accept that the play being written here is not under your direction. Watch him and love him. No, Mariel, you cannot go in or the girls will lose both parents.*

It was overwhelming to watch somebody I love in such peril without any physical way to help, but that is what I did. My trickling tears and oozing blood did not distract me from my connection with Stephen's ever smaller and more exhausted form. I was aware of the girls' whispered prayers beside me and the choked emotion we were holding back. The agony went on and on. I must have spent fifteen minutes trapped in the undertow. Stephen was battered for at least twice that long. In the end, he was released by the most unlikely savior we could imagine—a great mother of the waves, the largest and most awesome of the day. We held our breath in a collective gasp as it broke right on him, burying him from our sight under tons of water. I thought he was down for good, a feeling that grew as the time stretched out to impossibility.

Sharp-eyed Dree saw him first. We were looking too far out. Like a piece of flotsam, he was down in the wrack near the rocks that saved me. "He's there. He's got a rock!" The currents had pushed him to the same blessed rock I had clung to. Like me, he struggled to find a grip, and eventually was heaved up on the flat surface by the force of a wave. We had the green stains from that rock under our fingernails for weeks. He was stripped totally naked by the waves, his bathing suit, shirt, and bracelet joining his hat somewhere on the sea floor. He looked beautiful and shiny hunched over the rock, like a seal. His elegant hands were playing at skimming the water. He was so out of it that he seemed to have forgotten that his rock was getting smothered by the bigger waves, another one of which might be along any second. When he finally got to his feet, his face showed no joy or relief—he was deeply in shock.

The girls and I were elated. I worked my way out near him while the girls ran for his spare shorts and sandals. Our hero made it home. We were wordless on our walk back to what now seemed a very different private cove. Sitting in the sand, we girls all wept while Stephen tried to get his breath. His heart was pounding in his skin. I just looked at him and felt tremendous gratitude.

I still feel the gratitude here in my yoga studio. I enjoy, truly enjoy, the luxury of *prana*—deep, slow breath—imagining that I am light, but solid at the same time. I have shifted my Eagle pose to the right foot, and that forms the solid core connecting me to the ground. The masculine effort of my right side is thoroughly entwined with the feminine surrender of the left. It reminds me of the unconscious balance I achieved when I began successfully working my way through the surf without fighting. I spread my toes and pull up on the calf muscle. The sensation of lift rises through me until I find lightness in my breath. I round my back—fluff my feathers. I am birdlike and winsome. For this moment, at least, I have found the right balance of acceptance and work, effort and surrender. I move to the left side again, to make balance there. My feminine side is easier, so I'm able to tune my wings more subtly into balance. The left leg and foot engage into the earth. With Eagle pose gently taken on this side, I can piece together our ocean experience. As I stared out at my drowning husband, I knew that I could not save him then, and it occurs to me that I can't do it now, either. There is no part of his journey that is mine except a shared history and circumstance. Neither can my hero man save me from my dangers and my demons. My journey, too, is my own. The two of us are blessed to have our separate lives to share together, but no partner, child, or teacher can complete or heal me. We are our own saviors.

A perfect balance

A SAMPLE YOGA ROUTINE

The sequence of yoga postures introducing the chapters of this book was determined by the demands of my story. I don't think I would ever do a real practice in that order. So, in the interest of saving you dear readers from various forms of confusion and back strain, I want to close by suggesting a more normal, rational kind of daily practice.

CAT AND DOG TILT

Instruction:

- Come onto all fours, aligning your knees directly below your hips, hip-distance apart, and your wrists about an inch in front of your shoulders, shoulder-distance apart.
- Draw your shoulders down your back and spread wide across your chest. Feel your breath.
- Open and spread your palms into the Earth, spreading your fingers wide apart and pressing the entire span of your palms, knuckles, and fingers firmly down.
- Inhale and lift your sitting bones, dropping your belly toward the Earth as you extend your chest forward and up (gazing either up or down, depending on how your neck feels). This is Dog Tilt.
- Exhale and press more firmly down into your hands. Round your back toward the sky, feeling your belly draw toward your spine as your breath flows out. This is Cat Tilt.
- Continue for five more cycles, feeling your breath initiate each movement, gradually deepening the two stretches.
- In the Dog Tilt position, feel your spine drawing through toward your chest (heart center) as you draw your shoulders down and back and lift your sitting bones higher.

- In the Cat Tilt position, feel your belly draw toward your spine as all of your breath flows out, drawing your forehead and pubic bone toward each other.
- After five cycles relax back into Rabbit pose for five deep breaths.

Benefits:

- Cat and Dog Tilt will help you to begin connecting your breath to movement in your body.
- It also stimulates spinal fluid and the digestive tract, loosens the neck and shoulders, gently stimulates the back and abdominal muscles, awakens the spirit, and creates a feeling of inner connection with your body and breath.

2

DOWNWARD FACING DOG

Instruction:

- Moving slowly and consciously, staying with your breath, bring yourself onto all fours, with your knees beneath your hips, hip-distance apart, your wrists below your shoulders, shoulder-distance apart.
- Spread your fingers wide apart, middle fingers pointing

straight forward, and press firmly down into the entire span of your palms and all of your knuckles.

• Draw your shoulder blades down your back and lightly in toward your back ribs.

• Curl your toes under, take a deep breath, then, exhaling, straighten your legs, shifting your hips up and back.

• See that your feet are parallel and hip-distance apart. If your heels are high off the floor or it's difficult to straighten your legs, then play around with separating your feet further apart.

• Keep bringing your attention back to your breath, to smooth, full, tension-free, complete inhaling and exhaling.

• Little by little, start to work the pose more strongly. Keeping your breath most important, start to bring more awareness into your roots in your hands and feet. Work from your roots...fingers spreading, more of your palms opening into the Earth, pressing all of your knuckles firmly down, especially the knuckles of your index fingers and the space from there to your thumbs.

• Feel how by pressing more into your palms, you can extend more through your arms, your sides, and spine, stretching your fingertips and sitting bones away from each other.

• Stretching your heels toward the floor, imagine there are literally roots extending from your heels into the Earth. As you spread your toes and root more firmly into your feet, firm your thighs, lifting your kneecaps and pressing the tops of your femur bones strongly back, cultivating more length in your spine through the strength of your legs.

• Keeping your inner arches and ankles lifted, (don't let the ankles sag) have a feeling of pressing the top of your ankles back into your heels, heels into the Earth.

• Stay for up to 5 breaths at first, eventually working up to staying comfortably in the pose for 2–3 minutes.

• Exhaling, come down onto your knees, point your toes back and release back into Rabbit pose.

Benefits:
* Develops strength in the hands, arms, shoulders, back, and legs; stretches the entire body; increases circulation; improves respiration; rejuvenates the body, focuses the mind, and awakens the spirit.

3

RABBIT POSE

Instruction:
* Standing on all fours, bring your knees hip-distance apart and your toes together.
* Release your hips down onto your heels and lay your chest down over your thighs.
* Bring your arms along the floor to your sides.
* Inhale deeply, then as you exhale allow yourself to completely let go. Release your forehead, shoulders, belly, and hips down toward the floor.
* Focus your attention on the simple and conscious flow of your breath, feeling the fullness each time you inhale and completeness each time you exhale.
* Slowly deepen your breath, paying more subtle attention to the beginning when you inhale, the ending when you exhale,

and the quiet spaces in between. Stay here for 1–2 minutes or longer.

Benefits:

♦ Relaxes and releases pressure in the entire body, especially in the spine, neck, and shoulders; massages and stimulates abdominal organs, soothing, calming, and rejuvenating; promotes a sense of ease and tranquillity. This pose should be used for resting anytime the practice feels too difficult.

4

MOUNTAIN POSE

Instruction:

♦ Standing with your feet together at the front of your mat, draw your palms together at your heart, close your eyes, and draw your awareness more inside. Feel your breath, soften your face, eyes resting lightly on a point in front of you.

♦ Little by little start to firmly press your feet down into the Earth, firming your legs, kneecaps lifting.

♦ As you inhale, draw energy more up through your core, gently lifting from your perineum and extending taller through your spine, your heart center lifting and spreading, the crown of your head extending toward the sky.

* Keep this extension and openness with you as you slowly exhale, relaxing your face, letting your shoulders draw down your back, your floating ribs soften in. Keep rooting your feet firmly down, as if through the floor and into the Earth, firming your legs, staying calm and relaxed in your face, your jaw, your eyes, your lips.

* Each time you inhale, feel your side ribs spreading and lifting, open more across your heart center, extending tall through your core.

Benefits:

* As the foundation for all standing poses, Mountain pose teaches the connected actions of rooting and extending, cultivates better balance, aligns the body.

5

(a)   (b)

SUN SALUTATION

Instruction:

* Come into *Tadasana*, the Mountain pose *(a)*.

* Take a deep breath. Exhaling slowly, release your arms

(c)   (d)

out to the side at shoulder height, turning your palms
up *(b)*.

* Inhaling, reach your arms out and up overhead; see your
  thumbs *(c)*. Exhaling, hinge at your hips and slowly swan-
  dive all the way forward and down *(d)*, leading with your
  heart, keeping your legs strong as you fold into a Standing
  Forward Bend *(e)*.
* If you feel strain in your lower back or hamstrings, then
  bend your knees as you fold forward.
* Inhaling, extend your torso forward, reaching long through
  your spine, and place hands on the floor, if you can *(f)*.
  Exhaling, step or lightly jump back to a plank position *(g)*
  with your arms straight and shoulders aligned over your wrists.

(e)   (f)

(g)   (h)

* If this is too much on your arms or if your midsection is droop-
ing toward the floor, then place your knees on the floor (*h*).

* Press the floor away with your hands, and if you are in the
full plank position, firmly press your heels back and firm
your legs as you did in Mountain pose.

* Take a deep breath, then as you exhale, slowly bend your
elbows until your shoulders are level with your elbows,
elbows to your sides, *Chaturanga Dandasana* (*i*, push-up
position).

[If you're unable to hold this position, then release all the
way to the floor. Press your hips and palms down into the
floor, press your tailbone toward your heels, keep your elbows
drawing toward your sides, and then inhale and reach your

(i)   (j)

(k)   (l)

chest forward and up, drawing your shoulders back and down, coming into the Cobra pose *(j)*. Exhaling, press back onto all fours and then lift your hips back and up into Downward Facing Dog. *(l)*.]

♦ From *Chaturanga (i)*, inhaling, extend your toes back and pull your hips forward as you press your arms straight, coming into Upward Facing Dog *(k)*.

♦ In Upward Facing Dog, firmly press your feet down into the floor, firming your thighs toward the sky, tailbone drawing toward your heels.

♦ From here draw the curve up your spine, shoulders drawing back and down as you lift and spread across your collarbones.

♦ Exhaling, roll over your toes and lift your sitting bones up and back into Downward Facing Dog *(l)*.

♦ Staying with your breath, keep inhaling and exhaling, cultivating deep, slow, full, rhythmic breathing while holding Downward Facing Dog for five complete breaths.

♦ Keeping your breath most important, keep coming back to your roots, pressing firmly and evenly down into the entire span of your palms, grounding your knuckles, stretching your fingers forward. See that your middle fingers are parallel and in line with your shoulders. Gradually root down more strongly and steadily into your heels, lifting your kneecaps, firming your thighs, and pressing the tops of your

(m)

(n)

thighs back to stretch your sitting bones farther away from your fingertips. Stay relaxed amidst the strength of the pose, working it as strongly as you can steadily maintain.

♦ Take in one more deep breath, stay to exhale it all out, then when empty of breath look forward and step or lightly jump your feet toward your hands. Keep inhaling, extending your spine forward as much as you can as you come onto your fingertips. Exhaling, fold forward and down into Standing Forward Bend *(m)*, keeping length in the front of your spine.

♦ Pressing your feet firmly into the Earth and inhaling, sweep your arms out as you come with a flat back all the way up to standing, reaching your arms overhead as much as you can *(n)*. Exhaling, draw your arms out and down, growing taller through your spine.

Benefits:

♦ Sun Salutation is the core of a flow practice. It generates heat in the body, enabling you to open up more easily in the postures to come. Its cardiovascular benefits enhance the heart and blood flow.

WARRIOR I VIA THE SUN SALUTATION

Instruction:

 * Do a Sun Salutation as described above, making your way into Downward Facing Dog pose.
 * Completely exhale and simply step your right foot forward to your right hand, knee directly over your ankle, left heel down, outer edge of your left foot rooting into the Earth.
 * As you inhale press more into your feet, reaching your arms overhead and extending straight up through your spine into Warrior I. Stay here, breathing. See that your right knee is aligned directly over your ankle.
 * Rooting more into the outer edge of your left foot, lift your left inner arch, and draw your left hip more forward and down, right hip drawing back, squaring your hips toward the front of your mat.
 * Extending straight up through your spine, take in one more breath, reaching up through your arms. Exhaling, swan-dive forward and down to *Chaturanga Dandasana* (push-up position), elbows grazing your sides.
 * Inhaling, move into Upward Facing Dog. Exhaling, move slowly back to Downward Facing Dog.

- Step your left foot forward, knee over ankle, right heel down, heart reaching forward, and, inhaling, coming up into Warrior I.

- Stay here, breathing, rooting into your feet, slight Cat Tilt in your pelvis, tailbone drawing down, creating more space between your left hip and thigh. Extend straight up through your spine, floating ribs softening in, heart center lifting and spreading from inside, extending your side ribs up away from your hips, reaching strongly up through your arms, and take one more breath in.

- Exhaling slowly, come down, trying to extend that breathing out all the way to *Chaturanga*, feeling *Chaturanga* as a pose.

- Inhaling, come to Upward Facing Dog, feeling your legs, buttocks toward your heels.

- Exhaling, press back to Downward Facing Dog, smoothing out your breath.

- Stretch into your heels, legs firm, sitting bones and fingertips stretching away from each other, shoulders spiraling outward.

- Take in one more deep breath, stay to exhale all your breath out, then when empty of breath look forward and step or float your feet to your hands, breathing in as you lengthen your heart forward. Exhaling, fold in to *Uttanasana*, the Standing Forward Bend, legs strong, spine long.

- Inhaling, press firmly into your feet and raise your torso with a flat back all the way up to standing, extending your arms overhead as far as you can; then, exhaling, draw your palms back to your heart.

- Repeat for a total of 3–5 cycles.

Benefits:

 • This posture strengthens your legs. It helps with deep breathing because the chest is open and expanded. The extended arms relieve stiffness in the neck and shoulders.

7

TRIANGLE POSE

Instruction:

- From Mountain pose, stepping to the right on your mat, place your feet three and a half feet apart.
- Starting with your feet parallel, turn your right foot out 90 degrees and point your right kneecap toward the small-toe side of your right foot.
- Turn your left foot slightly in.
- Extend your arms out to the side, level with the floor.
- Press your feet strongly down and firm your quadriceps muscles.
- See that your right kneecap is drawing up.
- Looking out over your right fingertips, inhale as you reach out through your right side as far as you can, getting the maximum extension in your spine as you press your hips to the left.
- Once you reach your fullest extension, draw your right hand straight down to wherever it naturally lands on your shin or ankle. (If your hand does not reach down to your shin, then use a chair for support of your hand.)
- Extend your left arm straight up, reaching up through your fingertips as much as you can. Keep pressing into your feet and firming your legs.

- Each time you inhale, cultivate more extension through your spine.
- Each time you exhale, open your torso toward the ceiling.
- Stay for 5−8 breaths.
- To come out of the pose, press firmly into your feet and, inhaling, reach through your left arm to come all the way back to standing.
- Repeat on the other side.

Benefits:
- This tones the legs and strengthens the ankles, as well as strengthening and opening the chest (heart center).

8

WARRIOR II

Instruction:
- Standing, separate your feet to four feet apart.
- Turn your right foot out 90 degrees and turn your left foot slightly in.
- Extend your arms out to the side and gaze out over your right fingertips.
- Pressing into your feet, take a deep breath in. Exhaling

slowly, bend your right knee directly over your ankle, with your knee pointing toward the little-toe side of your foot.

* Turn your palms up, draw your shoulders down your back, extend your arms away from each other, and simply turn your palms back over, breathing.

* Keep pressing into your feet, right foot spiraling energetically clockwise, left foot counterclockwise as you ground the outer edge of your right foot, lifting your right inner arch, right thigh pressing back.

* Keep extending up through your core and out through your arms and the crown of your head.

* Press more into your feet and, inhaling, slowly straighten your right leg. Turn your feet back to parallel and repeat on the other side.

* Stay for 5—8 breaths on each side; eventually work up to staying 1—2 minutes.

Benefits:

* Again, this tones the legs and relieves cramps and stiffness in the legs and hips. It also tones the abdominal muscles.

EAGLE POSE

Instruction:

* Stand in Mountain pose (see page 204). Focus your gaze and find balance while breathing, rooting, and extending.
* Slowly bend your knees a few inches and extend your arms out to the side.
* Lift your right knee up, cross it over your left knee and try to hook your right foot behind your lower left leg.
* Reach your arms forward and cross them over each other with your left arm on top until your left elbow is on top of your right elbow.
* Extend your forearms straight up and try to press your palms together.
* Try to sit farther down while lifting your torso away from your thighs.
* Try to lift your elbows up in front of your chin and press your hands away from your face.
* Stay for 5 breaths, eventually staying for 1–2 minutes.
* Repeat with opposite crossings on the other side.

Benefits:

♦ Eagle pose develops balance; strengthens the feet, ankles, and legs; and stretches the hip flexors, back, and shoulder muscles.

10

DANCER'S POSE

Instruction:

♦ Stand in Mountain pose (see page 204). Focus your gaze and find balance while breathing, rooting, and extending.

♦ Slowly bend your right knee and lift your right foot up toward your right hip. Reaching down on the outside of your leg, clasp your right foot with your right hand on the outside of the foot.

♦ Extend your left arm straight up.

♦ Take in a deep breath, then, exhaling, extend your torso and left arm forward while reaching your right leg behind you as high as you can. Let your gaze rest steadily out over your left fingertips.

♦ Try to rotate your right hip forward in order to bring your hips and shoulders to a position square with the front of your mat.

♦ Keep cultivating Mountain pose in your left leg while

pressing your tailbone down and drawing the curve in your back higher up.
* Either stay in this position or, if you can, rotate your right elbow out and up to clasp your right toes overhead.
* Slowly bring your left hand to your right foot, drawing your elbows toward each other and the crown of your head back toward the arch of your right foot.
* Hold for 5—8 breaths.

Benefits:
* This develops tremendous strength in the legs as it stretches the thighs and stretches and stimulates the spine. It also develops balance and mental focus.

BRIDGE

Instruction
* Lie on your back and draw your heels in toward your hips, hip-distance apart. Lay your arms on the floor at your sides. Take in a deep, full breath, feeling your side ribs and chest expand. Slowly exhale, feeling your ribs release. Notice that as all of your breath flows out, your belly draws lightly

toward your spine, pressing your spine gently toward the floor and causing your tailbone to tilt up slightly. This tilting action as you breathe out initiates your movement into the Bridge pose.

* When you are empty of breath press down into your heels and lift your hips off the floor, following your tailbone up as high as you can comfortably lift your hips.

* Interlace your fingers under your back and rock gently from side to side on your shoulders to shrug your shoulders underneath you a little more, thereby relieving pressure on your neck. Stay here for five breaths.

* Keep pressing your heels firmly down into the floor to extend your hips more toward the ceiling while pressing your buttocks toward your knees, thereby lengthening and protecting your lower back.

* Press more into the inner edges of your feet to keep your knees aligned directly over your ankles, to keep your inner thighs relaxing toward the floor, and to prevent tension in the sacrum.

* Bring your hands down to the floor, lengthen your arms and interlace your fingers, and continue to press down through your shoulders, elbows, and wrists, lifting your chest toward your chin as you press the tips of your shoulder blades through toward your chest and breathe.

* Hold for 5 breaths, then release the clasp of your hands and slowly roll down one vertebra at a time, with your sacrum the last to touch the floor.

* Keep your feet in place, let your knees come together, and completely relax for a few breaths. Repeat two more times.

Benefits:
* Promotes a healthy nervous system, thereby easing tension and releasing more energy; stimulates the kidneys and adrenals; stretches chest, shoulders, abdominals, and thighs. Promotes heart opening.

FULL WHEEL

Instruction:

- Lying on your back, place your feet on the floor in line with your hips.
- Place your feet so that their edges are parallel, which will give the sensation of being in a slightly pigeon-toed alignment. Let your knees rest together.
- Place your palms on your belly. Each time you inhale feel the natural spreading and lifting of your rib cage. Each time you exhale feel your ribs releasing in and toward the Earth. As all your breath flows out feel your belly draw down toward your spine.
- The next few times you exhale, press your breath completely out and feel your spine press toward the Earth and your tailbone curl slightly forward and up. This is the breath-induced internal action that you want to initiate your movement into Full Wheel.
- Staying with your breath, separate your knees until they are directly aligned over your heels.
- Place your hands on the floor just above your shoulders, shoulder-distance apart, palms down, fingers pointing toward

your feet. Point your elbows straight up toward the sky. Stay
as relaxed as you can.

♦ Exhale and, empty of breath, simultaneously press down into
your heels as your tailbone curls up *and* press down into your
hands, lifting your hips up and drawing the crown of your
head to the floor between your fingers.

♦ Stay here to take in another deep breath, drawing your
elbows toward each other and your shoulder blades in against
your back ribs.

♦ Exhale all your breath out, tailbone curling up, and, inhaling, press your arms and legs as straight as you can.

♦ Keep rooting firmly down into your heels to lift your hips
higher.

♦ Keep steadily pressing down into the inner edges of your
feet, keeping your knees over your heels and feeling your
inner thighs releasing down toward the floor.

Benefits:

♦ This develops strength and flexibility in the spine, shoulders,
and legs; stretches the entire front of the body, and is both
energizing and calming.

CAMEL

Instruction:

- Stand on your knees with your knees and feet hip-distance apart.
- Curl your toes under to lift your heels.
- Place your hands on your sacrum and press your sacrum down.
- Press down firmly into your knees and feet.
- Inhaling, lift your chest and draw the tips of your shoulder blades up toward your heart center.
- Exhaling, lean slightly back and place your hands on your heels, keeping your hips pressing forward and tailbone pressing down.
- Stay for 5–8 breaths.
- To come out of the pose, exhale completely, press more firmly into your feet and knees, and then, inhaling, lift through your chest while pressing down through your tailbone until your torso is all the way up.
- Repeat 1–2 times. For a deeper backbend, extend your feet flat on the floor, resting on your insteps.

Benefits:

◆ Camel opens the heart center and stretches the thighs, groin, and entire front of the body. It also brings flexibility to the spine, and stimulates the adrenals and kidneys.

14

SEATED TWIST

Instruction:

◆ Sitting on the floor, bend your left knee and, keeping your leg as close to the floor as possible, place your left foot by the side of your right hip. Cross your right leg over your left and place your right foot on the floor on the outside of your left knee.

◆ Revolve your torso to the right, placing your right hand on the floor behind you.

◆ As you inhale, reach your left arm up as high as you can and then, exhaling, extend it across your right leg as far as you can.

◆ Keep both sitting bones firmly rooted down and extend up through your spine as much as you can.

◆ Try to place your left shoulder across your right knee and then clasp your left foot with your left hand.

- Stay for 5–8 breaths.
- Repeat on the other side.

Benefits:

- The Seated Twist stimulates the abdominal organs (pancreas, liver, spleen, kidneys, stomach, and ascending and descending colons), helps proper digestion, and is useful in treating diabetes, constipation, and urinary problems. It also tones the nervous system, adjusts the spine, stretches the back muscles, and eliminates tension.

15

SEATED FORWARD BEND

Instruction:

- Sit on the floor and extend your legs straight out in front of you with your ankles drawn toward each other.
- If it is at all difficult to sit up straight or to straighten your legs, sit on a firm pillow or bolster to help you to maintain straight legs and spine.
- Firmly press your sitting bones down into the floor, flexing your feet and pressing the back of your legs firmly down into the floor.

* Keep extending as tall as you can through your spine. As you inhale feel your chest lifting and spreading.

* Maintaining as much length in your spine as you can, slowly extend your torso forward, bringing your hands to the floor on the sides of your legs. Keep your sitting bones rooted into the floor.

* Each time you inhale, extend more through the front of your spine, lengthening from your belly through your chest while gazing down and keeping the back of your neck long.

* As you feel more open and flexible, eventually clasp your shins, ankles, feet, or toes.

* Be sensitive to pressure in your lower back and release if you feel any sharp sensations in your spine.

* Hold for 1–3 minutes.

Benefits:

* The Seated Forward Bend lengthens and strengthens the spine; improves vital energy flow; stimulates abdominal organs, especially the kidneys; and refreshes the mind and emotions. The intense stretch of the pelvis region brings more oxygenated blood there, nourishing the reproductive organs. It is deeply relaxing and great for relieving anxiety.

SEATED FORWARD BEND WITH BENT LEG

Instruction:

- This pose begins the same as the Seated Forward Bend.
- Sit on the floor and extend your legs straight out in front of you with your ankles drawn toward each other.
- If it is at all difficult to sit up straight or to straighten your legs, sit on a firm pillow or bolster to help you to maintain straight legs and spine.
- Firmly press your sitting bones down into the floor, flexing your feet and pressing the back of your legs firmly down into the floor.
- Keep extending as tall as you can through your spine. Changing as little as you can, slide your right heel in toward your upper inner thigh.
- Press your heel into your thigh while drawing your right knee toward the floor.
- Be sensitive to any pressure in your right knee.
- Place your hands on the floor just behind your hips to encourage more extension through your spine while grounding your sitting bones firmly into the floor.
- Slightly turn your torso and chest toward your extended left leg.

* As you inhale grow taller through your spine and more expansive across your chest.
* As you exhale fold forward over your left leg, bringing your hands to the sides of your left leg or to your left foot.
* Stay with your breath.
* Each time you inhale, extend more through the front of your spine, lengthening from your belly through your chest while gazing down and keeping the back of your neck long.
* As you feel more open and flexible, eventually clasp your shins, ankles, feet, or toes.
* Be sensitive to pressure in your lower back and release if you feel any sharp sensations in your spine. Hold for 1 minute. Repeat on the opposite side.

Benefits:
* This stretches the legs, relieves tension in the lower back, elongates the spine, opens the hips, stimulates circulation through the spine, torso, and abdominal organs, and quiets the mind.

SHOULDER STAND

Instruction:

* If you are menstruating or tend to have strain in your neck, then do a *Half Shoulder Stand,* as follows:
  * Place a long bolster next to a wall, parallel to it and about a foot away from the wall.
  * Seat yourself on the bolster facing the wall by approaching it sideways, using your hands for support to help get into position.
  * Facing the wall, begin to lie back and extend your legs up the wall.
  * Lie down all the way, with your lower back and hips on the bolster, your head and shoulders on the floor, and your legs extended up the wall, ankles together.
  * Your arms may be placed alongside your body, palms down on your belly or up toward the ceiling, or you may bring your arms behind your head on the floor in the shape of a diamond (elbows out, fingertips touching). Stay for 1—3 minutes.
* To prepare for the *full Shoulder Stand,* lie on your back.
* Bring your feet over your head and onto the floor, curling your toes forward, and press your feet down.

- Interlace your fingers behind your back and press your arms, elbows, and wrists into the floor.
- Rocking gently from side to side, draw your shoulders under your body so there is less pressure on your neck.
- Raise your legs into the air while strengthening your thighs and pushing your hips up in line with your raised legs. Lengthen your spine by releasing your clasped hands, bending your arms, and placing your hands on your back as close to the floor as you can.
- Give support to your back with your hands and by pressing your elbows firmly down into the floor.
- Extend energy up through your legs, pressing your ankles together, spreading your toes, and pressing the balls of your feet up toward the ceiling. Allow your breath to flow steadily and calmly. Hold for 1—3 minutes.

Benefits:

- This strengthens and calms the nervous system and emotions by stimulating the thyroid and parathyroid glands. It is deeply relaxing and an excellent pose for overcoming insomnia.

CORPSE POSE

Instruction:

- Lie on the floor on your back, your body totally released and relaxed. Breathe naturally, with no tension anywhere in your body. Your arms are a few inches away from your sides, palms naturally open and facing up. Your legs are spread in a small V, rolling easily outward or wherever they are completely relaxed.

- In this very important relaxation posture your eyes are closed, yet your mind is sharp and aware of all that is going on inside you. Take note of your body and how it feels, while releasing into the posture any tension you may be holding on to.

- Maintain a sense of observation of your body and mind. Just watch as you feel the effects of your practice calming your mind.

Benefits:

- This pose relieves tension and releases any tightness you might have accumulated during your practice. It clears your mind and fills you with a sense of peace. Take this feeling of calm into your day. This is the perfect place to begin your meditation. You are relaxed and at ease and ready to sit in silence.

MEDITATION POSITION

Instruction:
- Sit in a comfortable cross-legged position.
- If your knees are higher than your hips, then sit up on a block, bolster, or folded blanket until your knees are lower than your hips.
- If you can easily sit in a simple cross-legged position with your sitting bones on the floor, try to place the top of your right foot on your left thigh close to the left hip and the top of your left foot on your right thigh close to the right hip. Be very sensitive to your knees in attempting this position and back away if you feel any strain in your knees.
- Root firmly down into your sitting bones and sit tall with your palms resting either in your lap or on your knees.

Benefits:
- This position allows one to sit still and free of physical distraction. It creates flexibility in the hip joint, strengthens the spine, and induces calm. My hands are in *Namaste,* or prayer position, at the beginning and end of meditation.

I use this time to say a prayer or to contemplate my intention for my meditation or how I would like to proceed throughout my day. You can choose to use this time for addressing your intention or focus as you see fit.